RADICAL
TENDERNESS

RADICAL TENDERNESS

The Value of Vulnerability in an Often Unkind World

GISELE BARRETO FETTERMAN

with Concepción de León

G. P. Putnam's Sons
New York

PUTNAM
— EST. 1838 —

G. P. PUTNAM'S SONS
Publishers Since 1838
an imprint of Penguin Random House LLC
1745 Broadway, New York, NY 10019
penguinrandomhouse.com

Title page art: background watercolor strokes © Innoria/Shutterstock.com
Book design by Laura K. Corless

Library of Congress Cataloging-in-Publication Data has been applied for.

ISBN 9780593852880
Ebook ISBN 9780593852897

Printed in the United States of America
1 3 5 7 9 10 8 6 4 2

The authorized representative in the EU for product safety and compliance is
Penguin Random House Ireland, Morrison Chambers, 32 Nassau Street,
Dublin D02 YH68, Ireland, https://eu-contact.penguin.ie.

For my Uncle Telmo.
The sun shines less brightly in your absence.

CONTENTS

INTRODUCTION

A RETURN TO TENDERNESS

1

CHAPTER 1

WE ARE ALL DESERVING OF TENDERNESS

11

CHAPTER 2

THE WORLD IS GOING TO EAT YOU ALIVE

41

CHAPTER 3

LISTEN TO YOUR INTUITION

65

CHAPTER 4

THE POWER OF COMMUNITY

87

CHAPTER 5

BARRIERS TO TENDERNESS

109

CHAPTER 6

PLEASE CALL ME SLOP

129

CHAPTER 7

REDEFINING STRENGTH

149

CHAPTER 8

WHY TENDERNESS = LEADERSHIP

169

CHAPTER 9

A TENDER FUTURE

191

ACKNOWLEDGMENTS

207

READING LIST

209

NOTES

211

INDEX

213

ABOUT THE AUTHOR

223

Even if, from the sky, poison befalls all
I'm still sweetness
wrapped in sweetness
wrapped in sweetness . . .
—RUMI

No more apologies for a bleeding heart when the
opposite is no heart at all. Danger of losing our
humanity must be met with more humanity.
—TONI MORRISON

RADICAL
TENDERNESS

A RETURN TO TENDERNESS

I n 2019, a women's collective in Pittsburgh invited me to lead a panel discussion on the subject of resilience. The panel comprised an incredible group of women—including authors, self-defense instructors, photographers, and others—many of whom had survived and thrived despite experiencing abuse, poverty, homelessness, or other hardships. It was part of a daylong conference dedicated to disrupters working to change the face of wellness and make the space more inclusive, accessible, and humane. The discussion was meant to be inspiring and nourishing, to show audience members a way into health that considered their varied identities and experiences.

The conversation was wide-ranging. Over the course of forty-five minutes, we talked about toxicity and harassment in the workplace, leadership styles, and the challenges of being a minority in all-white spaces. Most of the anecdotes and advice were laced with positivity, meant to inspire and motivate the women sitting in the audience, who were listening attentively. This was all as expected . . . but I kept feeling like something was missing.

It has always been fascinating to me that even in spaces that are safe, full of attendees who went in with a mutually supportive mindset, speakers often veer toward sharing stories of *triumph* rather than hardship—of getting over a hurdle rather than tripping on it. Don't get me wrong: I'm a bright and optimistic person. I lean toward the light, and I do not view my life through the lens of victimhood or struggle. I certainly didn't want the women to wallow in self-pity or sadness. But I did want to hear about how despair was released or how they dealt with moments when they wanted to break down. Their struggles. Their vulnerabilities. Their dark moments of the soul.

By then, my husband John was lieutenant governor of the state, which made me Second Lady of Pennsylvania—or, as I irreverently branded myself, SLOP. All of a sudden, I was very, *visibly*, in the spotlight. I was finding it hard to get used to the increased scrutiny and attention that came with the role, which had made me the target of vitriol and threats far beyond what John received. My status as a former undocumented immigrant, which I was open about and was shared on John's website, had become a subject of online trolling, with people calling for me to "go back to my country." People accused John and me of having a green card marriage, despite my already having been documented when we met, and commenters beneath his photos would ask him things like, "Where did you buy her? Where can

I buy one like that?" Other criticism ranged from frivolous—
"You dress like you're going to the club"—to scary, including
death threats.

And what I was starting to realize (which shows you just
how naïve I was!), was that my actions on this now-public stage
didn't just affect me, or even our kids. Everything—from the
clothes I wore to the charities I supported to the off-the-cuff
comments I made at an event—reflected on my husband, too.
Life in the spotlight frequently left me feeling raw. Exposed.
Vulnerable.

Likewise, the women all had a robust online presence. I was
curious about how *they* dealt with the sometimes-cruel criticism
and trolling they were surely subject to on social media. So, toward the end of the panel—after many fascinating stories of
these remarkable women's successes, triumphs, and well-earned
victories—I shifted the conversation.

"This is all so instructive," I said. "But what do you do when
things *aren't* great?" I looked around at the women assembled
before me. "Give me some tips. I want to learn." I wanted to get
at what was underneath the women's success stories, hoping they
would vulnerably let us all into the space between facing and
overcoming.

The women on the panel all offered strategies for responding
to or overcoming criticism. *Push back with facts. Make them listen.
Get in their face. Scream.* Their responses elicited applause and
excitement from the audience, around 150 women who had
come to the event to be inspired and absorb by osmosis the fearlessness and fierceness of the women leaders on the stage.

I didn't expect the question to come back to me in the end. But when it did, I answered truthfully.

"Me? I cry," I said. The words brought what had been a steady stream of affirming nods and finger snapping to hushed attention. I sensed a feeling of disappointment roll through the room. Attendees seemed to shift in their seats and cast glances about as if to say, *That's it? That's all you've got for us?*

I'd expected as much. Mine was an admission that many might feel embarrassed to make. One that likely didn't align with common perceptions of strength or resilience. It's the sort of vulnerability that is seen as a form of surrender, as if you are giving up, or giving *in* to the trolls.

But it made me ask myself: Was refusing to fight back *really* a form of surrender? Was it truly off-limits to talk about crying—much less shed tears in front of others (which by then had become something of a habit for me)? Did showing true emotion in the public sphere have to be viewed as shameful or cringeworthy? It certainly was rare: As a society, we're much more likely to admit to punching a pillow, or clapping back, or publicly calling out our trolls than we are to confessing that, well, this stuff *hurts* sometimes. And then to sit with (or even publicly reveal) those feelings.

People have been telling me to fight back for my whole life. But I don't need to fight. I don't need to be right. I have found a different approach, one that is authentic to me and that often leads to remarkable results. I show my feelings. I express my vulnerabilities. I'm not afraid to be soft, even tender, in the face of anger and hostility. But that's because to me, exposing this side of myself isn't weakness. It's my secret strength. Maybe even a form of rebellion.

To me, expressing and leading with tenderness is a necessary—and even *radical*—way of reclaiming the parts of ourselves we are forced to deny.

Tenderness as a Radical Act

After the panel that day, several women came up to me and admitted, in whispers, that they were criers, too, but that succumbing to tears made them feel like "losers." That stuck with me. Why are we so afraid of revealing our soft underbellies?

What I've realized is that, as a society, we mistake vulnerability for weakness or a lack of grit. We lean into toughness because we want to show the world we're not to be taken lightly. We want people to be wary of crossing us. We puff up our chests, we talk loud, we take up space in an attempt to intimidate others. "F—— around and find out," as the saying goes. So many of us—men and women—act like the vigor and aggressiveness with which we respond to a situation should be positively correlated with how others approach us. *The more you mess with me, the higher the chance you'll find out what I'm made of and get a piece of my mind. The greater your offense, the greater my response.* And sure, that's one way to go.

But it's never worked for me. Throughout my life, this mentality has hurt rather than helped me and the people around me.

What we *believe* will relieve our anger or pain—talking tough, lashing out, exacting revenge—often boomerangs back into our bodies, eating away at us like a termite in an otherwise healthy tree. Hurling unkind words as a show of strength is not the panacea many perceive it to be—at least it has not been for me. I believe that the more goodness we spread into the world, the more likely we are to receive it in return.

It's a radical—even extreme—idea to many. And when I bring it up to others, it often raises the question: *Then, how do I protect myself?*

It's a valid point, especially considering the many ways, both physical and emotional, in which our society's collective traumas turn to mutual destruction, ping-ponging from one person to another and spreading like a disease. We poke at one another's pain points, hoping that it will relieve us of a sense of helplessness. And the expectation of this, of having to dodge these attacks, causes many of us to walk around with our guard up, ready to pop off at the slightest sign of an insult or injury. How else will we stop others from taking advantage of us? Better to walk around with protective armor than to leave an opening for others to hurt us. Better to be feared than to be exposed.

These messages seem to prevail everywhere I look—in television shows and movies, in profiles of successful businesspeople, in politics, in our treatment and expectations of survivors of abuse and assault, in the workplace. We glorify those who seem impenetrable; those who "survive" and overcome, who seem to face challenges without any outward expression of having crumbled. People like this—tough, stoic, unflinching—are viewed as worthy of respect and admiration, their rock-hard exteriors a sign that they have what it takes to cut it in our harsh world.

But I do not believe that is the only way to be. I never have. I am a soft girl by nature—as you'll see, even as a young girl I preferred consensus over conflict. But none of us are unchangeable. Even if the world has made us tough, I believe there are real benefits to approaching the world with vulnerability and tenderness—and that we can *all* move in that direction by choice.

I want to challenge the perception that expressing emotions like sadness or disappointment or fear is a sign of weakness. Instead, it is our strength. It is our protection. It is what will save us.

A Different Way to Move Through the World

I am not suggesting that we all reduce ourselves to a puddle of tears and refuse to deal head-on with life's challenges. The opposite, really: I am suggesting we learn to sit with hard things, adapt when needed, and spread tenderness in a world that would have us remain hidden and disconnected. It takes openness and strength to feel the sometimes-difficult emotions that so many of us tamp down each and every day.

But I focus on the importance of tears because they are the first expression of pain we learn to suppress. Even small children, all of us—especially boys—are reprimanded for or discouraged from crying. Parents justify this by saying they are preparing their kids for the world, but really we are teaching them an early lesson in self-silencing and establishing a toxic framework for approaching adulthood. It's a lesson that reverberates throughout our lives.

Let's eliminate the phrase "fighting back tears" from our vocabulary. Let's not start by fighting our own bodies. Instead, we should consider reframing our thinking around what tears mean and how these can serve us. In a recent documentary about her life, the iconic poet Nikki Giovanni discussed how she coped with a challenging childhood by suppressing her feelings. But she acknowledges the importance and difficulty of learning to cry. "I automatically wipe / My eyes even though I know / Crying / Is a skill," she said, reading from her poem "I Married My Mother." It's one we should all relearn.

Crying is strength. It helps us set boundaries. And most important, it can be a stopgap until we are ready to act or react. I reject the idea that we should shoot our pain inward to survive. The world will not change if we are expected to keep silencing the voice inside of us that tells us things should be different. And the world *needs* to change. As does how we define strength. The simple acceptance of tears can be a precursor to radically reimagining what it means to be respected, strong, and resilient. Softness also takes strength.

It's my mission—through exploring the role of tenderness in my own life and uplifting other examples of vulnerability in work, family, and life—to show that big feelings are nothing to be embarrassed about. That gentleness can be a superpower, not a liability. And that embracing our emotions and leaning into vulnerability is not a form of weakness, but rather a strength— one that is critical to social and cultural change. Doing so can transform the way we lead, treat one another, and prepare future generations to build a better, more empathetic world.

CHAPTER 1

WE ARE ALL
DESERVING OF TENDERNESS

Tenderness, I believe, is inherent in all of us. Think of young children: sweet, earnest, wide-eyed. Naturally, some retain it more than others. Some of us are more in tune with our inborn sensitivity, our warmth, our compassion. But at our core, when we are safe and well taken care of, we are capable of and lean toward softness.

At least that's what I believe and how I've lived my life. It's when we are exposed to people and situations that demand toughness that we lose that side of ourselves. I was lucky to grow up in an environment and intergenerational home that embraced my tenderness.

I was seven when I landed in New York City in December 1989, a child-sized suitcase in tow. My mother, who I call Mamãe, had come to the United States ahead of my brother and me, and we followed soon after with Bibi, my grandmother. My mom was newly divorced from my stepfather, and Bibi explained that we would be flying on an airplane to a new land that would offer a fresh start. But what does that mean to a child? All I knew was that I was shivering, ill-prepared for the blistering cold in my canvas sneakers and summer clothes. I remember vividly that I arrived at John F. Kennedy Airport nursing a broken fingernail that had been torn off by a car door before I left Brazil. Those physical sensations—an unfamiliar chill in the air, a throbbing finger—are ever present in my memories of that time.

I did not fully understand then that we would not be going back home, in my case for a long while, and in my mom and brother's case, not at all. It had all happened so fast. Back in Rio de Janeiro, Mamãe had only said that we were going on an adventure. She had told us to pack our things, instructing us to take only what felt important. I struggled to decide what to pack, because everything felt valuable. My favorite teddy bear. My first doll. A diary. Some clothes and books. I figured I would eventually go back for what I left behind. But for decades, I would not set foot back in Brazil.

Once my mother made the decision to leave, determining this was the best path forward for our future, she quickly severed all our physical ties to Brazil. She sold our home and furniture and resigned from work. She made it so that we had no choice but to go, locking herself into the move. And after a few months in the United States, we had overstayed our tourist visas and become undocumented, which meant we had to stay if we wanted to make the United States our permanent home. Leaving would have made it difficult for us to come back.

My life in the United States was markedly different from my life in Brazil. In Rio, I had lived in a neighborhood called Tijuca, where we grew sugarcane and coconut in our junglelike backyard and sometimes saw monkeys climbing the trees outside our window. Uncles and cousins lived nearby and would visit often, and the whole family gathered weekly on Sundays. My earliest memories were of a warm, boisterous family and spending weekends and afternoons running around with my feet in the dirt or swimming and rollerblading with my cousins and friends.

In New York City, our first home was Jackson Heights in Queens. We were surrounded by neutral-colored homes, red-brick buildings, and a thundering overhead train. Under the dark, loud tracks, vendors sold food and products from the neighborhood residents' varied cultures—authentic tacos from Mexico, arepas from Colombia, pupusas from El Salvador. My family arrived at the apartment of a friend of a friend of my uncle's, a fellow Brazilian woman who lived with her husband in Queens and let us crash with her until we found an affordable rental of our own. We did not stay there for long, but for the time we were there, they fed us and never made us feel like we were intruding. That is how many newly arrived immigrants survive—through community, kindness from strangers, bonds forged over the shared experience of leaving behind the only home we knew. People we may never have met open their homes, wallets, and workplaces to help us settle into life in a new country, and then we pay it forward. Arriving in a community where schoolchildren and neighbors spoke a variety of languages and were comfortable with difference made transitioning into life in the United States a lot easier. No one in Jackson Heights looked at my family with suspicion. Our differences united us.

The transition to America must have been challenging for Mamãe, though she never let it show. In Brazil, she had been an accomplished professional woman who had earned multiple advanced degrees in education and nutrition and ran multiple hospital nutrition programs. But in the United States, her undocumented status made her educational achievements useless. She found a job as a housekeeper, working long hours to make ends meet, and sometimes I would ask her to take me with her. I'd help with small tasks like vacuuming and wiping down counters but spent most of my time roaming the halls of the big fancy homes she cleaned, in awe of American-style luxury.

Though my brother and I were too young to quite grasp our change in social standing, thinking back, I can recognize the ways in which we were treated differently compared to Brazil. I remember the way people stared at my mom when she walked around with her caddy of cleaning supplies, or when she stumbled over words while speaking English. Or, once I had mastered English, how they would direct questions at me even though she was fully capable of answering them. It was clear that some folks looked down on her for her accent and line of work. They would lose patience with her if she couldn't explain herself or raise their voices as if this would help overcome the language barrier. In Jackson Heights, we were able to blend in and be seen as equal members of the community—there were plenty of other Brazilian immigrants, and particularly in the 1990s it was very much an economically and culturally diverse part of New York City. But when we were in primarily English-speaking spaces or in neighborhoods where few people looked or sounded like us—dark featured and clearly foreign—the same did not always prove to be true.

I remember one time, on the way to the beach, my mother was pulled over. I do not recall the context of the stop—it could've been a routine check or a broken taillight—but I do remember the officer's attitude toward my mom. For context: My mother learned English quickly and was fluent. She had a heavy accent, of course, which is often the case for people who learn a new language as adults, but she had taken night classes and was an ace at Scrabble. Her vocabulary was extensive. But the officer was impatient during the entire interaction. He kept asking her to repeat herself in an annoyed tone and looking back at us kids, silently requesting that we step in as translators. I was frozen in place because I was so afraid of cops, but my mom stood her ground. She was firm and calm as she handed over her license. She did not let the officer's frustration faze her and, rather than get flustered, she worked to get her point across until the officer was satisfied.

Despite some isolated incidents like this, our lives never once felt sad or tragic. On weekends when she wasn't working, Mamãe, my brother, and I would "get lost" across the city, getting off at random train stops to explore our new surroundings. We wandered around parks and crashed parties (once at a fire station, which would prove prophetic); we window-shopped or popped into thrift stores. Mamãe always used language that made any activity feel exciting. Dumpster diving or curb shopping was going on a "treasure hunt"; getting lost was a "game." We were not undocumented migrants stumbling through the unfamiliar and often forbidding city. We were adventurers exploring a new land.

We learned quickly that the United States did not suffer the same lack that we had witnessed in Rio. On garbage days, the streets would fill with furniture discarded in near-mint condition. Coming from a country where many people lived in extreme poverty and kids often didn't have shoes to wear, my mother struggled with how wasteful it felt to toss things that still had life in them. So once we finally got our own place, it was not uncommon for us to pick up some of these discarded items off the street to furnish our apartment. All our furniture was worn and mismatched or, as some politely commented when they visited, *eclectic*. But it was clean (or at least, we could make it so with a little elbow grease), and as Mamãe reminded us, it was the right price—free.

About a year after relocating to the United States, we moved again, this time to Harrison, New Jersey—a working-class immigrant community just over the Hudson River, less than an hour's drive from Queens but seemingly a world away from the busy city. We were just starting to get the hang of living in Jackson Heights, but Mamãe had heard from a Brazilian couple that the Garden State was better than New York City for raising kids, so once again we packed up and settled somewhere new. That's how, the summer before I started third grade, my brother and I landed in a new school and town, living in a railroad apartment above a Peruvian restaurant. In old pictures, my brother and I are seated at our dining room table, folding newspapers that my mom would sometimes deliver around the neighborhood as a part-time job.

On my first day at my new elementary school, my grandmother Bibi and I walked there hand in hand. Mamãe was typically out of the house early, so Bibi was usually the one who got us up and ready for school. She fed me breakfast and fresh-squeezed orange juice and helped me pack my book bag. I was a bundle of nerves and excitement during the ten-minute walk to school. I worried about what could go wrong and wondered whether I'd make new friends. My English was still rudimentary at best. My clothes weren't cool. I also didn't look like a lot of the other kids—at nine years old, I had a unibrow and long hair that had never been cut, because Bibi wanted to maintain the loose curls that formed at its end. "If you cut it, you'll lose them forever," she'd often say.

Bibi played an oversized role in my life, always protective and doting. She did not like the idea of me walking anywhere alone, so she would insist on walking me to friends' houses or anywhere I needed to go, even if it was close by. Once we arrived, she'd go inside to meet my friends' parents and make sure I would be in a safe environment. Bibi was a sucker for a good laugh, and she would often tell jokes or play pranks on us, like taking out her dentures to embarrass us in public or tease other kids. I remember her always dancing around the house to old Brazilian music, which I loved.

She was also incredibly generous, both with us and with everyone she knew. With what little she had saved for retirement, she sent money back to her godson in Brazil, who had special needs. She did this all her life. Bibi was super creative and always saved random containers, scraps of fabric, buttons, and even the plastic fasteners used to secure bags of bread, for art projects or other functional uses. Her expectations of us were high—I still hear her voice in my head snapping at me to correct my posture—but she was also generous with compliments and words of affirmation. She often told me I was beautiful and sweet and loved.

Even to my young mind, our new town of Harrison was very different from New York City. There was no subway and the streets were wider. Like Jackson Heights, Harrison had a significant immigrant community, but most transplants had arrived from Europe—Ireland, Poland, and Portugal. I don't remember seeing any Black people, and though there were Latinos from Peru, Brazil, and other parts of Latin America, they were represented in much smaller numbers compared to Jackson Heights. On the way to school, rather than bodegas and apartment buildings, we passed houses, churches, and lots of bars.

Once we arrived, the principal helped me register and gave us a tour before guiding me to a classroom. Handing me off to my new teacher, Mrs. Barnhill, he introduced me saying, "This is Gisele. She's from Brazil." I said hello and took my seat.

That's when Mrs. Barnhill faced me and said something I've never forgotten: "Wherever you came from, however you got here, I'm so glad to see you." That simple phrase—an open-handed welcome—melted away any nervousness or stress, making me realize I was at home in that classroom and school.

Over the next year, I excelled in math but struggled for a bit with other subjects that required English fluency. My classmate Sandra, whose family was Portuguese, sat with me and helped me translate when I was having a tough time understanding lessons or directions and would get discouraged. I remember being frustrated that I couldn't figure out what the teachers wanted from me, but I was also reluctant to admit my confusion. To betray that I was struggling felt like a weakness. I hadn't yet learned about the power of vulnerability.

But Sandra understood instinctively what I needed. She, too, was living in an intergenerational home and being raised by a strong mother and grandmother. "It's OK that you don't understand right now," she said to me. "This isn't forever." Sandra was my accomplice in "faking it until you make it." We regularly drew the Keds logo on our off-brand canvas shoes, making do with whatever our parents could afford for us. I've never forgotten her simple kindness, and we're still friends to this day. She was one of my first guides in the art of tenderness.

The Safety to Be Soft

That welcoming environment at Lincoln Elementary extended beyond just Sandra and Mrs. Barnhill, and I thrived there. The school had English as a second language classes and buddy programs for non–English speaking students, and there were even some signs in Portuguese. In my head as a kid, these accommodations were just for me. Soon, I joined the color guard and, in addition to Sandra, made other friends who remain in my life to this day. I loved school. It was from being so thoroughly accepted there—and particularly from internalizing Mrs. Barnhill's words on that first day of school—that I learned to be a welcomer in my later years. It is a skill that I would carry with me, almost obsessively, for the rest of my life. I never wanted someone to feel as isolated and frustrated as I'd felt in those early days.

Even though I felt a sense of belonging in Harrison, where I would spend the rest of my childhood and teenage years, I missed my family and life back in Brazil. Like most immigrants, I grew up searching and yearning for home, reminiscing about the parts of me I had left behind. I missed my uncle, Tio Telmo, the most—he was one of the most important people in my life, a former intelligence agent and bonus father figure. He was the cool uncle, always wearing button-down shirts with a few buttons undone and a gold chain. Like his mom, Bibi, he was a jokester, always in a good mood and fun to be around. He made friends easily and was able to disarm the grumpiest of people. Tio Telmo was also generous—he always said, "Money is like blood, Gisele. It needs to keep moving." He would take me to concerts and, whenever he would visit the United States, we would go to unlimited crab leg buffets and stay there as long as we could, eating, talking, and laughing. I desperately wished he could be with me all the time, like he was back in Rio.

Compared to our time spent in Brazil, our lives in the United States were more self-contained, our circle smaller. We kept in touch with family members over the phone and later WhatsApp, and they would sometimes visit us in New Jersey, but it was not the same. Being an immigrant means living with a broken heart; rarely will everyone you love be together at the same time.

What we lacked in community, Mamãe made up for in her effort to make sure we lived full, enriching lives. She saved relentlessly to take us on trips across the country—to Disney World, Texas, and California. It was important to her that our lives felt limitless. Autonomy and independence were qualities she valued and instilled, and she would never tell us anything was out of reach. On a recent trip to New Orleans, I encountered a Latino family on vacation. They were still learning English, wore fanny packs around their waists (all five of them!), and had cameras around their necks. I overheard an emotional moment between them in which they shared that this trip was a stretch for them, but it was clear that it had been worthwhile. They were having a great time, smiling and pointing out all the amazing sights and sounds of that gorgeous city. Watching and admiring them, I found myself full-blown crying in the streets of NOLA. I saw my own Mamãe in their proud matriarch, bustling her kids around the town, determined to give them everything they deserved. I was aware of the hard work that likely went into such a trip, the expense and planning and scrimping and saving. I was reminded of the trips I took with my family as a kid. I wondered if people who looked at us back then saw what I did. I really hope so.

I was thoroughly cared for, cherished, and protected growing up, and I only realized later how rare that is. Like other immigrants, I grew up in a multigenerational home, with my grandmother Bibi staying with us for long stretches over the years, in between visits back to Brazil. She wasn't like us. We overstayed our visas and became undocumented. But Bibi refused to do so. She would always travel back and forth, maintaining her connection with the people back home.

Looking back at my childhood, I know intellectually that Bibi must have been gone a lot as she split her time between the United States and Brazil, but the funny thing is I don't remember her ever not being there. She was the one to greet us after school when Mamãe was working. She'd help my brother and me take off our backpacks. She would feed us grapes that she had carefully peeled and cut in half, because she was afraid of pesticides, and also didn't want us to choke. (She continued to do this for me well into my late thirties!) It was one of the many gestures of love shown to me by Bibi and Mamãe—some downright peculiar as I reflect back on them today, but all rooted in their care and concern. I vividly remember that they worried about me using the toilet paper at school because "What if it had rolled onto the floor?" So Bibi sewed me a toilet-paper-roll-shaped purse, in which I'd carry my own wherever I went. Oh, and just to be sure I didn't lose it (and that everyone knew who it belonged to), she embroidered my name in bright pink letters on the side. (Imagine raising your hand to go to the bathroom in middle school and heading there with a toilet-paper-shaped bag in tow. The thought of it still makes me laugh.)

But there were other gestures, too—each small and thoughtful. Bibi made my brother and me birthday cakes every year, decorated with a delicate white meringue. She was a talented seamstress, and in addition to the toilet-paper purse, she also sewed and tailored many garments for us over the years. When I was little, she made us matching outfits, using the same fabric to make dresses for me and shorts for my brother. As for my mom, anytime I call or ask her for a favor, she drops everything to make me feel heard or to follow through with my request. She's never brushed me off, whether my questions or concerns were a little bit or big important.

This is what we all need, especially in our early years: safety, acceptance, and love. Feeling seen and embraced both at home and at school created space for me to freely be who I was, which in my case was a big softy. What we receive in our early years is not in our control, and I was certainly lucky, but I believe we can all create that sense of safety for ourselves.

How We Learn to Silence Our Feelings

Maybe because home was a soft cushion, I have always had and embraced big emotions. I was never explicitly shut down or told to stop crying or feeling. But even so, the lessons in staying quiet, staying in line, and silencing my emotions came early. While Mamãe indulged us, she never let my brother or me forget that, as undocumented kids, we had to move through the world differently from our peers. We did not have insurance to protect us in medical emergencies, and if we got in trouble, it was unlikely we would be treated with the same leniency our peers might have received. That's why, before I left home every day, my mother always reminded me that we should strive to "be invisible" and not draw too much attention to ourselves. It was her way of keeping us safe.

I probably internalized the "be invisible" messaging more than my mother intended. She meant to instill caution rather than fear. (When I talk to her about it now, she says, "Gisele, you were never in danger of getting deported.") Her faith and firm belief in the right to start over as many times as needed guided her to believe things would work out.

But in my mind, deportation was a looming threat. Everyone around me knew a family that had been touched by deportation, and that knowledge rattled me. Once you know someone who's been deported, it feels that much closer. I was always scared the same would happen to me if I wasn't careful and felt a pit in my stomach anytime a police officer or an authority figure seemed poised to approach me.

Decades later, even the family we lived with in Queens was separated by deportation. By then, they had two sons and owned a home and a business. They were, to my mind, very American. But after decades in the country, both parents were deported and given a ten-year penalty for their undocumented stay in the United States. The immigration officials had come and taken them in the middle of the night, leaving behind their teenage, U.S. born kids. The older one was barely eighteen and was left to care for his fifteen-year-old brother, relying on the kindness of non-relative adults to help them through. Though their parents would eventually return, these two teenagers were essentially left to fend for themselves before their time.

Because these stories were not uncommon, I lived on edge, acutely aware of our undocumented status. I was always careful not to get hurt or draw too much attention. Once, when I was nine, I broke my nose playing kickball in gym class. My family could not afford medical treatment, so rather than go to the doctor, I just adjusted to not being able to breathe well. By the time I got it fixed in my thirties, my nasal wall had collapsed and had to be rebuilt. I didn't lament not being able to go to the doctor regularly as a kid—it was just the way things were.

I knew I couldn't have all the experiences my friends had. Once, when my school planned a ski trip to Canada, I lied and said I couldn't make it that weekend, even though the real reason was that I couldn't travel to another country, since I didn't have a U.S. passport or documentation. And of course, I was never able to get together with my uncles/aunts/cousins like so many of my classmates did—my sprawling family was a continent (and an impossible trip) away.

Mamãe, who moved to the United States and never looked back, did not walk through her new country with fear. She believed everything would be fine if we just did the "right" things— paid our taxes, did well in school, stayed out of trouble—but I was terrified of being sent back to a place I no longer knew.

One day in middle school, I stayed home sick. At some point, the doorbell rang. Bibi and I looked at each other and stayed quiet. Neither of us was expecting anyone, and we were nervous to see who was trying to find us. Out the window, we saw my vice principal. I freaked out. I figured he had to have been there for something serious. Was he there to deport us? In that moment, I thought about what I would have to pack and about how sad it would be to leave my friends behind and make new ones back in Brazil. The worst part was the wondering.

For the rest of the day, I was on edge and tried to run through what his reasons could have been for visiting my home. Had I done something wrong? What would happen the next day at school? I was in a total panic. But he never did approach me, and I never found out why he showed up at my door. I know now, of course, that deportation would not have come by way of a school official. But as a preteen, all I saw was a powerful person who might have discovered my secret, and it frightened me. I thought my life in the United States was over. My status was a bogeyman looming over my childhood, a constant source of stress that kept me on shaky ground.

By then, my memories of living in Brazil were fading, and I relied on stories and anecdotes from adults to paint a picture of life back in my home country. I remember my mother and her friends sitting around the kitchen table discussing what was happening back home. Who was mugged or had fallen into poverty or been hit by another tragedy. Once, a cousin was carjacked, and even though he surrendered his car and keys, which is what people are trained to do there, he was still shot. His recovery was brutal, and he would never again walk without a cane. Most families in Rio have their own version of this story.

While we had been upper middle class in Rio, the vast inequality made anyone and any neighborhood susceptible to crime. The violence never felt far away.

Shortly before we left Brazil for the United States, Mamãe had a conversation with my aunt that solidified her decision to emigrate. In discussing the violence in the city, her sister-in-law remarked, rather flippantly, that the situation was getting better, because out of seven times she'd been mugged that year, "only four had been at gunpoint." The casualness with which she said this chilled my mother. She knew she did not want her children to grow up in an environment in which violence was normalized. She did not want to see us surrender to the violence or live in the uncertainty of whether one of her children might not make it home. She left behind her education and her career, even knowing that living in the United States with limited English skills would be arduous. She once told me she would "clean houses for the rest of my life" if it meant we would be safe.

Many immigrants (and Americans, too) have this sort of story. Imagine coming from a place where you lived in constant fear that you or a family member could be physically harmed, or even killed. The mental and emotional stress would be tough for anyone to bear, especially a child. So many arrive in the United States with this sort of trauma, and yet life forces them to immediately jump into survival mode, just like Mamãe. There is no time for emotions or reflection when you're focused on subsistence. Which is probably why, for all the love that I felt in the working-class community around me, I didn't see the traits of tenderness or vulnerability celebrated much in my day-to-day life. Quite the opposite.

It was not uncommon in my neighborhood for fights to break out over seemingly minor conflicts. Once, in high school, a girl wanted to fight me, claiming I had kissed her boyfriend. (In fairness, I had . . . but I did not know he was her boyfriend at the time!) Still, my friends explained to me, justice must be done.

There was a tree a block away from the school building that served as the meeting ground for these adolescent confrontations. My classmate demanded that I meet her there at 4:30 p.m. after school. I didn't want to fight; in fact, I didn't even know *how*, and the prospect of throwing fists or bloodying noses terrified me. I'm sure many other teenagers feel the same way, but they find themselves forced to put on a show of bravado to save face. But this was not an environment that a softy like me knew how to navigate. When my classmate came up to me and yelled that she'd be waiting by the tree, I started crying. "But I don't know how to fight," I said. She was so taken aback that she called it off.

Years later, I'd learn about Maslow's theory of human motivation, and some of the toughness I grew up around started to make sense. Abraham Maslow was a psychologist who, in the 1940s, posited that the basic human needs were like steps on a ladder. Only after basic needs like food, water, and safety were met could humans move up the pyramid to touch the other needs like friendship, self-esteem, and "self-actualization"— what he defined as the pinnacle of personal growth and discovery. To be self-actualized, as defined by Maslow, means to become all you are capable of becoming. It is to know and understand yourself well, and to have the freedom, safety, and autonomy to live to your full potential, as the best version of yourself. Self-actualization is not exclusively tied to a profession (though professional success can play a part) but rather to a way of engaging with the world that allows you to experience it fully, building lasting and meaningful relationships, experiencing joy and awe, and having space to be creative and think expansively. But people who must focus their energy on making a living to cover the basics had little hope of fulfilling more complex needs.

This theory really spoke to me. It explained why, perhaps, so many of the working-class folks I grew up around did not have the capacity to think about therapy or feeling their feelings. Why they didn't have time to be soft, to be tender, to be vulnerable. Instead, people like my mom and grandmother developed a thick skin to cope with life's challenges. So many of the people I grew up with were walking up stairs that were far steeper than their legs could bear.

Once we came to the United States, Mamãe's life didn't instantly get better. In fact, her undocumented status often made her vulnerable to being cheated out of her pay or underpaid; she was once even assaulted, cornered in a bathroom by her employer while she was cleaning. When she told me the story, I was shocked and asked her what she did. "What do you think I did? I sprayed him in the eyes with Windex and ran out of there!" she said. She carried on because she had to. She had no other choice.

But toughening up isn't all it's cracked up to be. We deserve more than the bare minimum. And while putting up a wall, on its face, might protect us in some ways, it blocks us not only from connection with others but also our own inner lives. We deny ourselves the most basic need of all: empathy.

Find a Home for Your Feelings

It's true that part of growing up means leaving behind the emotional extremes of childhood. We learn not to yell when we're angry, not to cry hysterically when we're hungry, and not to lash out when we're upset. If done the right way, this training helps kids grow into adults who can communicate well with others and express their emotions without causing harm. But let's be real: How often do we *really* encounter these kinds of adults? More often what we learn in childhood is not regulation, but suppression and shame. We bury our hurt and trauma, hoping it becomes undetectable to others, living in a state of denial. Yet these feelings often have a way of creeping up and coming through even if they're unspoken. Unhealed pain is passed on to others.

It is probably widely understood at this point that the only way to overcome feelings is to work through them, but still there is so much resistance to vulnerability in our society. It's apparent in how children (and particularly boys) are encouraged to be tough and impenetrable; in how we're discouraged from crying in public and sometimes even private spaces. From an early age, those of us who don't align with the aggressive nature of the world are forced to put on a brave face or alter our personalities. In *The Myth of Normal: Trauma, Illness, and Healing in a Toxic Culture,* Dr. Gabor Maté's tome on the physical and emotional cost of our toxic social and economic culture, he writes that people are groomed "to fulfill our expected social roles and take on the characteristics necessary to do so, no matter the cumulative cost to our well-being." He calls this "separation from self" one of the central features of so-called normalcy in our society, serving to uphold social expectations.

I know this to be true because of the way my sensitivity was perceived and responded to growing up. I was a weeper, and in fact the same teacher who had made me feel welcome when I started school wrote to me on Facebook decades later that she remembered me as the dark-haired girl with a long braid and tiny voice who was "always crying." As a result, both at home and among friends, I was often told I needed to toughen up and develop a thicker skin if I was going to make it—in business or in life. It made me want to hide the most tender parts of myself. I thought I needed to change so I wouldn't be perceived as weak and, also, so I could avoid feeling alone. Especially as a kid, it feels easier to fit in than it does to stand out. Feelings sometimes felt embarrassing and like too much, and I got the sense that there was something wrong with me for not adapting to a world that demanded toughness, especially from young women of color.

For my mother, her circumstances required toughness. She

always stood up for herself and did not avoid conflict or cower when life dealt her a difficult blow. Unlike me, she did not walk around fearful because of her undocumented status, nor did she respond by shrinking in front of authority figures, whether it was the boss who attacked her at work, the police officer pulling her over, or school officials who gave her sass. Once, she got a letter from my teacher informing her that I was absent from school for a couple of days, but the wording of the letter seemed to imply that I had cut class. She went mama bear on them, writing back, "Yes, I *know* my daughter missed school. She had an audition, and I know because I drove her there!" I don't know that I would take such a firm tone today, let alone when I was undocumented. In my life, I don't think I have seen either my mother or grandmother cry or say they were afraid.

It took me a long time to realize that though I was different from my mother and grandmother, that did not mean I was not also strong or resilient; these traits just looked different on me. I was not a weakling because I did not want to fight. I just wished I was not expected to fight at all. Over the years, it occurred to me that perhaps it was not me who needed to change, but rather a world that demanded so much harshness. Whether in romantic or business relationships, it is often those of us who are gentle or sensitive who are asked to adapt to our environments. *We* are wrong for not wanting to live in a constant state of confrontation. For not adapting to such an exhausting way to live.

I came to realize that placing the burden of change on those who've been harmed is a form of victim blaming, rooted in our collective discomfort with vulnerability. I still hear, sometimes, "Gisele, you're too out there. This is too much." But I believe that everything we refuse to accept or feel lives with us. You can't heal what you do not feel.

I found a home for my feelings in *Mister Rogers' Neighborhood*, the long-running educational television show hosted by Fred Rogers. When I first came to the United States only speaking Portuguese, Mr. Rogers taught me English. But even more importantly, he was one of my first models for leading a tender life. Even today, it is the only programming in which I've ever felt at home. My family and I would watch his show with closed captioning (so I could see the words in English as well as hear them), and we'd record it on VHS for repeat viewing. I couldn't miss it. I felt such a deep connection to him. He was so deliberate and thoughtful—never rushing the words out of his mouth. And those slow words were *powerful*. Mr. Rogers taught me that you can say hard things in a gentle way. On the show, he taught children how to deal with issues they could be facing at home or school (like divorce, grief, or bullying) as well as those they were exposed to on the news (like war and civil rights demonstrations), helping them cope with and understand what they were seeing and hearing.

After Martin Luther King Jr. and Bobby Kennedy were killed, Mr. Rogers explained through a puppet what the word "assassination" meant and how to cope with grief. During the Vietnam War, he presented the conflict in simple terms using imaginary characters. In response to nationwide protests and acts of violence aimed at keeping Black and white people from swimming in the same pools, Mr. Rogers shot a scene in which he washed his feet in the same basin as Officer Clemmons, a recurring Black character, and allowed him to share his towel. No one else was talking to children about these subjects. As I was figuring out a new language (and, at the same time, looking for cues on how to be a good person), he was right there with me. He taught me that words matter, and tone is important. Even today, friends often say to me, "You just said something that was a real truth, but in a way that was nice." Mr. Rogers taught me that.

Mr. Rogers's message that everyone is special also resonated deeply with me. But after witnessing the social shift my mother experienced when she moved to the United States, I realized that simple message did not live within everyone. After my parents divorced shortly after I was born, Mamãe was briefly remarried to a successful businessman who moved us into his lavish home in Brasília. Her new husband owned a chain of pharmacies, and we got to experience life in a wealthy family. We had security guards, a driver, and a private chef. On weekends, we'd visit his ranch, where I learned to ride horses. Doors were opened for us and respect was assumed because of my stepfather's social status. Similarly, my mother's career and educational level granted her a certain level of respect from others.

But in the United States, though she was the same person— kind, considerate, intelligent—her job as a housekeeper brought her down on the social ladder. Her place in society was not determined by her ability, personality, or actions, but rather by how her job was valued within American society. The only thing that had changed was my mother's geography and the cultural values that surrounded her; everything else about her was the same. Moving through spaces now with people who believe themselves to be important, it's hard not to recognize how tenuous and arbitrary these attributions can be.

In the documentary *Won't You Be My Neighbor?*, Mr. Rogers's wife, Joanne Rogers, said that she and her husband both grew up in households in which it was not acceptable to express anger, and that Mr. Rogers was passing something along to children that he had not had access to himself. I believe my mother and grandmother broke similar generational curses in raising me. Bibi grew up in an impoverished, abusive home where she wasn't taught healthy expressions of love. By my mother's generation, our family's physical conditions had improved, but social conditions still weighed on us.

The field of epigenetics teaches us that pain is carried in families until someone is ready or able to feel it. Pain demands to be felt eventually. In her book *Break the Cycle: A Guide to Healing Intergenerational Trauma*, the Dominican American psychologist Mariel Buqué writes that this form of emotional trauma "transcends generations and could be experienced by multiple members of your family." Intergenerational trauma can be inherited either biologically—if your parents lived through negative experiences that fundamentally altered their genetic code—or through behaviors and practices. My mother and grandmother, who experienced trauma through their interpersonal and social experiences, were both "cycle breakers," as Dr. Buqué refers to those who choose to metabolize internalized trauma and change learned patterns, and they created an environment that allowed me to continue on that journey.

Mr. Rogers died on my twenty-first birthday. I still remember where I was when I heard the news—at home in Newark, getting ready to go out and celebrate with my friends. His death shook me profoundly; I actually stopped celebrating my birthday for several years, because the date reminded me too much of him and my sadness at his death. I never met him, of course, but I was mourning the loss of what he represented—compassion, love, and gentle goodness. There are few people or characters who so completely embody a spirit of tenderness and vulnerability the way Mr. Rogers did. And in moments of crisis, such as after 9/11, it was these traits that so many in our country turned to him to model.

In a 2002 commencement speech at Dartmouth College (one of his last public appearances before his death the following year), he shared some words about what his message of tenderness had meant over the years. "When I say it's *you* I like, I'm talking about that part of you that knows that life is far more than anything you can ever see, or hear, or touch," he said. "That deep part of you that allows you to stand for those things without which humankind cannot survive. Love that conquers hate. Peace that rises triumphant over war. And justice that proves more powerful than greed."

I believe his message was exactly what we needed, then and now. To this day, after I watch something intense on television, like a crime show, I sometimes throw on an episode of *Mr. Rogers* as a palate cleanser. Sort of like smelling a bag of pungent coffee beans after inhaling too much perfume.

Once I left Harrison, when I entered the "real world," I would encounter many people who seemed to be carrying a heavy burden—a burden that sometimes manifested itself through actions like biting remarks, overzealous anger, and even cruelty. This was a shock to a young girl like me, who had grown up with a lot of love, and whose default setting was tenderness rather than toughness. But the quality and quantity of love I received in my childhood—especially from my grandmother and mother, but also from so many in my school and community growing up—sustained me. In some ways, I think that my loving childhood inoculated me against certain types of unkindness as I got older.

In Brazilian Portuguese, there is a word, *cafuné*, that refers to the act of caressing or tenderly running your fingers through someone's hair. Anytime I would go crying to Bibi about anything, big or small, she would lay me on her lap and embrace me in a *cafuné*, saying, "Gisele, who cares what anybody says about you? You only give love because that's all you have inside of you. People who are giving something else out, that's what's inside of them. And isn't that so sad?"

After that, no matter what, I could only see people being unkind as being sad. I would create these elaborate stories in my head to accept them. That their parents did not hug them or their grandmother starved them. It helped me see them as someone in pain. Someone who is healthy and happy and in a good place, I reasoned, doesn't go out of their way to be mean to other people. More likely than not, there is a pain they're not engaging with, accepting, or facing—whatever it may be. And imagine, I would tell myself, carrying that all the time.

Bibi died during the pandemic, following two of her children who were casualties of the coronavirus. She was just shy of ninety-five years old, and she'd seen multiple generations of descendants grow up, bouncing between New Jersey, Brazil, Pennsylvania, and North Carolina to spend time with her scattered family members. Bibi did not seem to fear death. She used to joke that if she stayed in motion, it would be harder for the Grim Reaper to catch her. And whenever someone died who was younger than she was, she would say, "Can you believe someone cut in front of me?" She maintained her sense of adventure and zest for life until the very end. She went zip-lining for her ninety-first birthday, and right after she landed, the first thing she said was, "Wow, that was so cool!" In the last days of her life, we recorded an episode together for *Faxina*, a Portuguese-language podcast that features the unheard stories of Brazilian housekeepers living in the United States—one that I still go back and listen to just to hear her voice. In it, she talked about the traumas she herself had endured throughout her long life.

She had grown up with a wicked stepmother—a woman who would force steaming hot boiled eggs into her mouth and threaten to kill her if she told her father about these abuses. Bibi escaped to boarding school far away from her hometown, where she was cared for by French nuns, whom she credits with saving her. She married in her teens, to a traveling salesman who would leave home for months at a time. But her troubles didn't end there. On the day she went into labor with her last child, Bibi learned that the woman next to her in the delivery ward was also carrying her husband's child, so she divorced him. She raised four kids as a single mother, relying on nothing more than her sewing skills and working nonstop to make a living.

I heard these stories a lot as a child. Bibi would repeat them over and over, adding new details in each retelling. Despite all the challenges she faced, Bibi responded with aplomb. She clawed herself out of situations that threatened to tear her down and was brave enough to set off on her own during a time when this was neither expected nor easy for women. No matter what life threw at her, she did not back down. I do not know that I would have been able to do the same. But even though Bibi was tough—you did *not* want to mess with Bibi—she was also incredibly tender and loving with us. Every time I listened to these stories I was reminded and grateful for Bibi's care—for the love she was able to give despite not receiving it herself. Bibi taught me that we are all capable and deserving of tenderness. That all we had to do was try.

CHAPTER 2

THE WORLD IS GOING TO EAT YOU ALIVE

As I moved into my teens, I started to see more clearly why my family and friends warned me that my kindness could prove to be my weakness. I had always been told that I would get hurt if I did not toughen up, which to them meant learning not to let things get to me, not leaving an opening to be taken advantage of, and hardening myself to the harshness of the world.

It was difficult, though, to approach the world with the thick skin and brash attitude that many of those around me seemed to think it required. I had already had some exposure to what they were trying to protect me from. After all, I rode the New York City subway and sometimes encountered men who grabbed or catcalled me. Once, I witnessed a violent fight on a station platform in which one person was knocked down, and no one went to check on him. I was also a runner and knew that women did not have the luxury of going out for a run without running through an extensive safety checklist first: *Is it too dark out? Should I carry pepper spray? Will the park be too secluded?* I did not wear headphones on my runs because I knew I needed to be aware of my surroundings.

Still, I did things that some might reasonably consider reckless. As soon as I got my driver's license at eighteen, for example, I started picking up hitchhikers—people walking with heavy groceries or walking alone down a dangerous street. Sometimes, when people got in, the first thing they'd ask is, "Are you a cop?" It was the only reasonable explanation to them for why I would pick up a stranger. But I just loved talking to people and hearing their stories. How did I keep myself safe, you might ask? I would just playfully say, "You're not a serial killer, are you?" Worked every time. Most people were just having a rough day and were grateful for the ride. (I kept this up in Pennsylvania, and when I became Second Lady, the state troopers' first order of business was to tell me, "Mrs. Fetterman, as of today, picking up hitchhikers has to stop.")

I never told anyone what I was doing back then. To those who cared about me, my emotional vulnerability and niceness put me in danger. "People aren't like you, Gisele," they would say. "Not everyone is so nice." And if I wanted to survive intact, they reasoned, I shouldn't be either.

Certainly, I saw signs of brutality all around me. Once, as an older teen, I accompanied a friend to an abortion clinic, where we were met by a large, rowdy crowd of anti-abortion protesters. The callousness with which they yelled at us as we tried to make our way inside always stuck with me; I could not fathom that level of cruelty. Later, in college, I would volunteer as an escort for patients at an abortion clinic to support people like my friend. At school, a preoccupation with pride and respect often manifested in petty fights and confrontations (like my own brush with the girl whose boyfriend I kissed). People seemed to always be looking for an opportunity to prove how tough they could be. I also knew from watching television, reading books, and consuming media that softness was neither present nor celebrated in most spaces.

Still, your world is smaller when you're young, so I did not give much thought to what I might face in the "real world." My sensitivity was embraced and accepted by my close friends and family, so though I understood myself to be different, it had not yet proven to be a bad thing. For the most part, I was never bullied or targeted (at least I don't think so—who knows what people were saying before I learned to speak English). And if someone did not make me feel good, I could simply choose not to be their friend. There was also a level of reinforcement for tenderness in high school—those who got into fights or misbehaved in other ways often faced consequences for their actions. Between a nurturing school environment and a safe home sphere, I experienced a level of protection and insulation that I took for granted as a young person.

When I started working as an older teen, though, those training wheels came off. As much as adulthood brings freedom, it also brings limitations. You cannot choose your boss or your coworkers or your clients, especially not early in your career. It was jarring to see behavior that I understood to be problematic be normalized . . . and to realize that there was often no accountability for people, especially men, who behaved badly out in the world or in the workplace.

One of my first jobs in high school and through college was as a brand ambassador, which essentially means I was contracted with an agency to hand out promotional materials or swag during events for companies like Presidente and eBay. Sexual harassment at these promotional events was rampant. During nearly every shift, there were drunk men who made lewd comments on my appearance or tried to hit on me, even when I was underage. They'd say things about my legs, face, and outfits that are hard to imagine going without consequences today, though the issues persist.

One of my gigs during high school was to participate in meet and greets at toy stores across New Jersey dressed in the likeness of a newly released "Latin Barbie," in a floor-length Pepto-Bismol hued gown and a white sash. Little girls would attend with their parents to take pictures with me or get my (Barbie's) autograph. More than once, adult men would come to the events without their children. Though they often claimed to be there on their kids' behalf, my intuition told me otherwise. Would their child really be that excited about seeing a picture of their dad with Barbie instead of them? Even at seventeen years old, I knew this behavior was weird and icky. But I didn't yet have the words or skills to set limits or push back in a way that felt natural or empowering to me. I was slowly becoming attuned to the ways in which my gentle nature could potentially put me in danger.

Another source of uncertainty and possible danger was my status as an undocumented person. Since I'd arrived in 1989, my brother, mother, and I had flown under the radar with regard to our official status in the United States. We had overstayed our visas and were not legal residents. Thankfully, public schools did not require that we be legal residents to enroll, so my brother and I did not have any barriers to elementary or secondary education.

But as I got older, my biggest looming question was, What would I do after high school? Come senior year, like so many of my friends did, I wanted to apply to college and think about future careers. At that age, you want to know *something* is coming. And I was intelligent, curious, and eager to have some stability, to make some money, to find my own American Dream. I also knew that my family and teachers at school were rooting for me, and I did not want to let them down.

But as an undocumented person, I lived in a state of limbo, not knowing where I was going to land or what my options really were. Could I even apply to college? Could I go if I got in? How would I pay for it? All my dreams or goals felt limited by my immigration status. I knew I wasn't eligible for financial aid. I wanted to enlist in the military, but there was no pathway for me to do so. Even jury duty, which many view as no more than a hassle or inconvenience, was aspirational to me. I felt American and accepted by those around me, but my status was a weight keeping me grounded. *You are here, but you are not one of us. We may welcome you, but we cannot claim you.* I was hyperaware of the ways in which my life was unsettled, and how easily

I could have the rug pulled out from under me. Uncertainty felt normal.

When the time came to apply to colleges, I looked for affordable programs that I could pay for out of pocket. I enrolled at Kean University, a public institution, in the fall of 2000, which would allow me to pay per credit. Because so much of my time and energy needed to go toward paying for tuition, my memories from college are mostly of rushing to the next place—to work, school, home, and repeat. I generally was not sticking around after classes were over or participating in school activities or events. Still, I have always been a sociable person who enjoys talking to new people, so I took any opportunity I could to make friends, chatting with people in the few minutes while people were settling in before class or whenever I had a day off. I also made friends through random interactions outside of school; I would keep in touch with people who sat next to me on planes, and I once even built a friendship with a representative I talked to on a customer service call.

At Kean, I majored in math, hoping that I might be able to join the military and work in cryptography. I've always loved puzzles and solving problems (I'm an ace in Sudoku!). But since I knew joining the military was not an option because of my undocumented status, and I did not see many other paths for a math major besides being a teacher (which I knew I did not want to do), my dream began to shift. I was living in Newark, New Jersey, and had started to become aware of the inequity that existed within the nutritional education space. I began to feel drawn to my mother's line of work. So, in my senior year, less than a dozen credits shy of graduating, I decided to enroll in a certificate program at the Institute of Integrative Nutrition, which at the time was housed under Columbia Teachers College, to study nutrition, hoping to use my skills to address the need that I was witnessing around me.

By then, I knew myself well enough to understand what I needed from friendships and how I expected to be treated, so the people who were close to me embodied the traits that I sought to put out into the world: kindness and gentleness. If there was a time when my tenderness was questioned or taken advantage of by friends or in romantic relationships, it has not stayed with me. Whenever disagreements did break out in our friend group, I would play the role of peacemaker, encouraging others to talk through whatever issue was troubling them or me. Even back then, I had a bit of a kindergarten teacher vibe, saying things like, "Let's be better versions of ourselves!" or "Let's be kinder to each other!" Nothing ever felt big enough to really fight over. But I would soon learn that this approach is harder to pull off in the workplace, where power dynamics often force vulnerable people—those at the entry level, women, people of color—into silence.

Hello, Cruel World

I worked my way through college, continuing my brand ambassador work until I completed my certification in health counseling in 2004. That year, I became a permanent resident, which was a relief after such a long time trying to stay under the radar, and landed a job at a management consulting company, providing financial audits for our clients (those math classes paid off!). The work was perhaps not the most interesting stuff in the world, but it felt good to master a job, to get to know my colleagues, and to bring home a paycheck that was more than I'd ever earned with my brand-ambassador gig work. But what I encountered in office settings was a shock to my system.

Office life, it seemed to me, gave people like my former playground bullies and neighborhood tough guys free rein to be as harsh as they wanted to . . . and get praised for it. The environment (at least in this office) could be toxic. I recall my colleagues constantly yelling at junior people in the organization over seemingly minor mistakes—a typo in a report, a mis-scheduled appointment. A more grievous error could result in hysterics; I remember one missed deadline causing a reaction in a forty-year-old man that reminded me of a tantrum by a toddler. It was wild—like the workers had skipped the part of childhood when you learn emotional regulation.

On one occasion, there was a coworker who was struggling with a death in the family and her productivity at work slipped. Even though upper management was aware of her situation, she was unceremoniously let go, with what seemed to me little empathy. There had been no offer of support or an attempt to understand her situation on the company's part. Instead, one day, without warning, she was called into our boss's office and came out with a sullen expression. Everyone's eyes were glued to the papers on their desk as she packed up her things. And just like that, she was gone, and everyone continued working as if nothing had happened. It all seemed so cruel.

Being a young woman meant that my experience was also often tainted with sexism, as well. On one occasion, my boss invited me to a meeting with C-suite executives. As an entry-level employee, I was excited to be asked, even if I was just being called in to take notes. My assumption was that the invitation was a reward for good work. When I arrived, I was one of a handful of women in a room full of men. The top executive started the meeting and explained the company business we were there to discuss. Then, he inexplicably added, "And Gisele is here because I like to look at her."

This was long before Me Too, when behavior like that was still accepted (or at least ignored) in the workplace. So rather than audible gasps at such an offensive comment, there were scattered chuckles around the room. No one—not even the other women—corrected him or contradicted him. I felt humiliated and objectified but did not feel empowered to respond. I just remember thinking, *This is normal?*

My early experiences in the workplace set me on a path of really trying to understand how and why this kind of crude and cruel behavior had become so normalized. And, if it was having this kind of effect on me, what must it be doing to our society at large? In Gabor Maté's book *The Myth of Normal*, he contends that systemic inequities that have been accepted for so long by society as "normal"—poverty, sexism, racism, cruelty— are actually making us sick. "We have become accustomed—or perhaps better to say *acculturated*—to so much of what plagues us," he writes. These issues we see around us every day have become, he says, "for lack of a better word, normal." Yet, he adds, "those features of daily life that appear to us now as normal are the ones crying out the loudest for our scrutiny."

Yes! This really spoke to me. If the default expectation in the working world is that loud, tough, and brash are valued qualities, then it is often women who suffer most under the brunt of these expectations—in large part because the traits that are devalued (like empathy, tenderness, and kindness) are typically coded as feminine.

As such, workplaces can be hostile spaces for women. McKinsey & Company's 2023 *Women in the Workplace* report, conducted in partnership with LeanIn.Org, called the workplace a "mental minefield for many women" because of the microaggressions we experience in these spaces. For women with traditionally marginalized identities, "these slights happen more often and are even more demeaning," according to the report. "Women who experience microaggressions are much less likely to feel psychologically safe, which makes it harder to take risks, propose new ideas, or raise concerns," the report authors explain. "The stakes just feel too high."

Instead, women are expected to bear maltreatment or bullying—or dole it out—if they want to succeed. The report said that 78 percent of women who face microaggressions adjust how they look or act as a way to shield themselves. Some feel the need to hide parts of themselves or their identities, presenting only a portion of their true selves to reduce uncomfortable or emotionally damaging experiences in rooms where they are one of few.

In meetings that I sat in on as a young professional, even women at the executive level were often spoken over or, even worse, had original ideas taken by male coworkers. When I would ask the women how they felt or why they tolerated it, their response would be, "It's just the way it is." They felt powerless to change the status quo, and speaking out could backfire or cause undue retaliation from others who benefited from keeping things as they were.

I'm able to approach others with tenderness because I do not flatten my own emotional experiences. I let in hurt, sadness, and joy in equal measure. Yet this emotional range is discouraged in a society that places more value on traditionally masculine traits rather than those perceived as feminine. Too many people approach life through the lens of domination and "winning," which supports a cutthroat environment in which success is meant to be achieved even at the expense of others. Everyone is in a race to be number one. Masculinity, dominance, and, therefore, superiority are defined in opposition to womanhood. We've all seen how displaying so-called feminine traits can open men up to ridicule, because to be manly—and therefore powerful—is synonymous with devaluing traits, characteristics, or interests that are culturally coded as feminine. This includes displaying vulnerability or emotion in public and professional spaces. Much of the toxicity we see at work, so much of what I experienced in those early days of my career, is directly related to social rejection of femininity and all that it represents.

Thankfully, the reexamination of hostility in our work and social environments is already well underway. A lot has changed from when I first entered the workplace, and much of the bullying and toxic behavior I witnessed in the late 1990s and early 2000s is no longer as widespread or accepted. In many industries and workplaces, there has been a real effort to open up to more perspectives and different working styles. In these places, tenderness and vulnerability are no longer the automatic career killers they once were. But there's a lot more work to do.

The World Is Not Tender

I bought my first house when I was twenty, in the Roseville neighborhood of North Newark, near Branch Brook Park. The house I bought was a multifamily and my mother lived in one of the apartments, helping to cover the mortgage. I was thrilled to have my own space but still be her neighbor—it was my way of returning the care she had shown me, and it was also comforting to have her close by.

Back then, loans were much more freely given. This was in the go-go early 2000s, before the housing bubble burst, and my friends were buying homes left and right. It seemed like the thing to do, and I found a light blue three-story multifamily home that had clearly been neglected for a while and that I could actually afford. The house had been repossessed, so I bought it at a sheriff's sale for little money up front and secured a low-interest loan. This place needed a *lot* of work, but it was rewarding to make something that had been ugly beautiful again. I remodeled the kitchens, had the top floor balconies resecured, painted all the walls, and redid the landscaping in front of the house, filling it with plants and colorful flowers. The furnishings were bright and cozy; I had a yellow couch that made me smile whenever I looked at it. After nearly a year of renovations, a neighbor came up to me and said, "I'm so glad you bought the house and were able to make it something beautiful . . . given what happened there." *What was she talking about?* I had no idea, until she told me then that someone had once hung themselves there.

The other reason that my house was so affordable was that parts of Newark were quite impoverished and under-resourced, with all the issues that result from those stresses. I wasn't aware then of all the social, economic, and cultural factors shaping my neighbors' lives. My little corner of North Newark was full of hardworking blue-collar families like my own. Both of my next-door neighbors were Latino families. On one side was a Peruvian family who always had parties in their backyard, and on the other was a multigenerational Dominican family—grandparents, parents, and kids all lived together. I loved the noise and the bit of chaos. There are so many neighborhoods where you're just a person who lives there, but North Newark felt like a place where just choosing to live there, investing in renovating a home, added value and made an impact.

But as I got to know the community better, I could soon see that many of my neighbors weren't getting the resources and support they needed. I became involved with the Big Brothers Big Sisters of America and was assigned to a girl named Destinee, who lived in South Newark. She was seven years old and lived with her mother, Lola, who had for years been waiting for a liver transplant and had to get dialysis on a regular basis. South Newark was starkly different from North Newark. There, poverty was more widespread and carjackings were common. I never felt unsafe, but people often warned me not to drive around there with my doors unlocked. There weren't supermarkets within walking distance, just corner bodegas that were great for a late-night craving but did not offer healthy, fresh food. Businesses did not see hers as a neighborhood worth investing in. I did not have an accessible supermarket in my neighborhood either, but I had a car, so the distance wasn't an obstacle. It was easy for me to drive to nearby Montclair. But for people like Lola or Destinee with more limited means, there were no options.

I spent as much time as I could with Destinee. We went to events organized by Big Brothers, at bowling alleys or the movies. I took her to the zoo. These were experiences that her mom was not able to provide for her, both because she didn't have a car and also because her health issues forced her to stay at home. Destinee and I were together multiple times a week. One day, we did a room makeover, painting all the walls in her room. It took all day, and I ended up sleeping over. Spending time with Destinee was one of the most formative experiences of my life. We had fun together, and it was an opportunity to reconnect with the giddiness and innocence of childhood. I remain grateful for the time we shared. Through her, I gained a sister.

Over the years, Destinee became her mother's caregiver, and I saw how their family remained in a cycle of poverty that became hard to escape from. Destinee was smart and wanted to study criminal justice, but anytime her mother got sick, she would have to drop out of school or quit whatever job she was working at the time to care for her. She was a person who had been abandoned by society, with insufficient support to withstand the whiplash of setbacks she continued to face into adulthood. What Lola lacked in resources she made up for in tenderness and love for her daughter.

Years later, reading Isabel Wilkerson's *Caste: The Origins of Our Discontents*, I would be reminded of the disparity I witnessed in Newark and the ways in which Destinee's life was limited by her circumstances. Wilkerson is admirable for her ability to simplify complex social issues and educate without inducing shame. She has the power to bring people in because she is learning alongside the reader. She does not claim to have all the answers, instead takes us along on her research journey.

Reading her book was a revelation for me. Wilkerson addressed racial disparity in the United States in a groundbreaking way, identifying it as a caste system on par with what exists in India, as well as with other systems of social separation like South African apartheid. She opened my eyes to the ways in which the arbitrary categories and social levels we have assigned to people are essentially all made up, and how deep this stratification goes. Wilkerson likens caste to an old house we have inherited, one we had no hand in building but in which we must live.

"When people live in an old house, they come to adjust to the idiosyncrasies and outright dangers skulking in an old structure," she writes. "The awkward becomes acceptable, and the unacceptable becomes merely inconvenient." The people who suffer most in this old house are America's "untouchables"— Black people primarily, but also anyone else who is deemed inferior: immigrants, brown people, Muslims, women of color, and so on. This caste system goes "unspoken, unnamed, unacknowledged by everyday citizens even as they go about their lives adhering to it and acting upon it subconsciously to this day," Wilkerson writes.

Though I would not read *Caste* until many years later, this disparity had already started to become clear to me. Being undocumented meant that my family was considered of a lower caste than other Americans, and my young adulthood expanded my understanding of others who had also been relegated to this status. My eyes also began to open to how quickly one's status could shift. I watched with horror the way Muslim Americans were villainized after 9/11, viewed with suspicion, harassed, and attacked for the actions of a few. And living in Newark, New Jersey, I was surrounded by people who had been chronically overlooked. The city was littered with dilapidated homes, and many lived below the poverty line.

This was before the Prudential Center was built, attracting big-name acts and events to the city. Before a new young mayor put a national spotlight on the issues that plagued the city. Back then, Newark was most frequently in the news for violent crime or local government corruption. There was widespread poverty, and the city had suffered population loss for decades. Many Newark neighborhoods, including mine, were then and are now food deserts, meaning that fresh food was not easily accessible to its residents. In addition to that, many of the people around me relied on food stamps—my neighbors were struggling to fulfill even the most basic needs. This remains an issue, and in 2022, when the state committed to investing $240 million to eradicate food deserts across the state, several areas in Newark were on its proposed list.

Living in such neglected communities can have adverse effects on residents. In a 2023 study about the emotional impact of living in a highly polluted neighborhood in Newark, researchers found that residents experienced "anxiety, fear and anger" about their living conditions. The neighborhood, Ironbound, is primarily made up of immigrants from Central and South America, and they described feeling unheard by politicians and local leaders. One participant who had tried to call City Hall to complain about environmental conditions said that "trying to call town hall is probably like trying to call the court in Newark. You just get nasty people . . . nobody cares." The residents believed they were subjected to these environmental hazards because "it's an immigrant community."

Residents of these sorts of neglected communities, often from traditionally marginalized groups, have reason to be wary or distrustful. For them, defensiveness or lack of vulnerability is often rooted in the desire for self-protection. When systemic social and emotional violence is a regular occurrence, defensiveness becomes a learned protective mechanism. Racism, sexism, and other forms of discrimination have become so entrenched in our daily lives that facing these has been normalized, feeling inevitable and immutable. These social conditions are a roadblock toward tenderness, because tenderness requires vulnerability. Yet for those among us suffering the most, those at the bottom of the caste system as described by Wilkerson, vulnerability can feel dangerous.

In such a world, it's no surprise that being nice is often viewed with suspicion or derision; it earns you labels like Pollyanna or naïve. The idea that someone could remain kind amid all of life's struggles (or when others inflict pain) doesn't make sense to people. They assume it must be inauthentic—that niceness is a façade for whatever true feelings are underneath.

That idea is all too common these days. In my high school yearbook, a classmate I thought I was friendly with had said as much in her final note to me. Amid the usual messages—like *This isn't goodbye, it's see you later* and *Keep in touch!!*—a classmate wrote: "I've thought you were a fake bitch for three years. It turns out you're actually just really nice."

I've learned that it's common for people to be wary and look at others sideways when they seem earnest or sincere. People let us down a lot in life, and we feel disappointed and hurt, so we respond by putting up walls to prevent it from happening again. It's natural to want to repay others with what we receive. We grow uncomfortable with people who don't operate that way, always believing there is some kind of agenda, wondering what's really going on.

Choose Your Hard

To be able to give and accept kindness, one must first work out our personal trauma that inhibits connection and empathy. This is, of course, easier said than done.

Resmaa Menakem, a brilliant therapist and expert on conflict and violence, describes trauma as "a wordless story our body tells itself about what is safe and what is a threat." In his book *My Grandmother's Hands,* he writes about the idea of "trauma ghosting," which he defines as "the body's recurrent or pervasive sense that danger is just around the corner, or something terrible is going to happen any moment." It's an affliction familiar to people whose daily environment or experience teaches them that they need to be on high alert to protect themselves from harm. Acting hard, being tough, showing no mercy or weakness—these are all trauma responses. And if you have grown up in an unsafe environment, these responses might actually make a lot of sense.

But the question to ask when you get to a certain point is this: Does this reaction still make sense? Is it working for you? Does anticipating an adversarial stance when you're facing a challenging situation (rather than approaching with an outstretched hand) help or hurt the situation?

Both approaches to life—defensiveness and openness—are difficult. Both come with risks. But rather than accepting things as they are and steeling ourselves against the harshness of the world, I argue that we should—and must—do the work of healing our own trauma, so that we can start to approach the world with kinder eyes. If we move through the world with the expectation that people will give us their best, they very often do. And along the way, I'm also gifting *myself* the gentleness I deserve.

Getting to a place of operating from tenderness is hard work. It requires that we turn inward and unlearn the trauma responses we have developed throughout our lives. This is not easy! But it's a matter of choosing your hard. As Menakem writes, "Healing involves discomfort—but so does refusing to heal. And, over time, refusing to heal is *always* more painful."

An idea that really resonated with me was Menakem's distinction between "clean pain" and "dirty pain." Clean pain, he writes, "mends and can build your capacity for growth," while the alternative is "the pain of avoidance, blame, and denial." Whereas the former helps us metabolize difficult feelings, the latter constricts and causes further harm. "When people respond from their most wounded parts, become cruel or violent, or physically or emotionally run away, they experience dirty pain," he writes. "They also create more of it for themselves and others."

Committing to the work of self-healing frees us, builds resilience, and gives us space to spread that healing to others. "Bringing a settled body to any situation encourages the bodies around you to settle as well," Menakem writes, explaining the importance of trauma healing in activist work. I've seen, for example, how tenderness inspires the work of community safety practitioners in neighborhoods plagued by violent crime as an alternative to harsh policing tactics. The people who work in these programs offer group therapy, conflict mediation, and other tools to help interrupt cycles of violence among those at the bottom of the caste system. They develop and draw on deep community bonds and cultural knowledge to reach those at risk of succumbing to the impulse to retaliate against violent crime. As the common refrain goes, hurt people hurt people, so if we can use kindness, compassion, empathy—all parts of a more tender approach to problem-solving—we can help heal the hurt and change people's lives.

I read with fascination, for instance, an interview in *The New York Times* with Demeatreas Whatley, a violence interrupter for the organization Cure Violence Global, who said that if there's a fight, he would approach the person who lost the fight before that individual goes to grab a gun. "You've got to calm him down and let him save face," Whatley said. "I tell him: 'I lost plenty of fights,'" before asking, "Do you want to lose at least eight years of your life because you lost a fight?" People like Whatley prevent a lot of tragedies by reaching people on a personal level and reminding them of the real consequences of gun violence. John Hardy, a senior program manager at Cure Violence Global, said that, generally speaking, the guys they work with don't actually want to shoot anyone. "Consciously or unconsciously, they want someone to talk them down," he said. They want someone to speak and listen to them, to understand them, and to help them find a way to see reason without losing social status or credibility.

In poor communities of color, despite the idea that gun violence is rampant, "the use of a gun to settle even petty disputes is not at all the norm," according to the *Times* article. "It is the norm among a very small group of individuals—mostly young, mostly men." That most of the perpetrators of gun violence are men is telling and rooted in the ways in which starting at a young age, they are encouraged to reject their emotions, conflict resolution, and vulnerability in favor of a forced bravado. Violence interruption work teaches them differently and helps them connect with their negative emotions. It teaches them a different way to show strength.

It's not wrong for people to be defensive or angry, but it's hard on them. Those feelings, when internalized and left unprocessed, merely serve as an additional load on top of everything else we carry. I've seen how people behave when they haven't addressed trauma, and I imagine it is heavy to go through life with that burden. Latching on to that state of living on edge adds fuel to an already raging fire, gives it oxygen to grow. We lose out when we walk around on defense. It's true that being tender opens you up to being hurt or disappointed, but I believe ultimately, it's a matter of choosing your hard—deciding whether you will be in pain from holding everything in or take on the risk of letting others reach you. Vulnerability can be a form of protection by helping you gather information, teaching you who to let in and who to keep out. And when it goes well, there is opportunity for connection, which humans desperately need. We miss out on so much by keeping our distance, all because we are afraid to be honest about how we feel or ask the same of others.

As I learned more about the world—its social divisions, toxic competition, and celebration of cruelty—I thought back to the advice and concern I had received as a child to toughen up. I began to wonder why the onus to change was placed on *me*. Instead of us trying to stop what makes someone suffer, we want the person who's suffering to change. I became more convinced that what was required of me was not to adapt to the social order, but to stand more firmly in my own tenderheartedness. I also started to question what it meant and took to be successful, and whether conventional professional success was something that mattered to me at all.

CHAPTER 3

LISTEN TO YOUR INTUITION

ad I been interested in a path of professional success defined by money or had more drive to climb the proverbial corporate ladder, I probably would have faced many more struggles with my innate gentle nature. I might even have tried to change myself in ways that didn't fit my personality or feel authentic. But I've never been a very competitive person. I certainly wanted financial security, but success for the sake of success had never appealed to me.

Years later, when I decided to run a marathon, people would often ask me about my target time or where I wanted to place. But I didn't care about any of that. I would always tell them, "Last place is also a place." I was content with putting on my running shoes every day and gifting myself this new and exciting experience.

The same is true in my work. I have never been ambitious for money or status. On the contrary, I was always drawn to public service. I wanted my work to be meaningful and touch others' lives. That's not to say that everyone I encountered in the non-profit space, which is where I'd end up, shared my commitment to tenderness. I certainly encountered people who felt them-selves in competition with other organizations and who engaged in bad-faith behaviors. On several occasions, people from orga-nizations with ostensibly aligned values bad-mouthed each other in front of me or refused to collaborate with one another for fear of losing credit. People were reluctant to collaborate with ventures that already existed because they valued owning something; cared more about being recognized than about the impact of the work. But I never felt threatened by seeing others succeed, so this mentality never resonated. As such, I avoided and did not engage in the same behavior, keeping my focus on the people I wanted to serve. Over the years, this attitude has sometimes made me a target for people who know I will not push back. Collaborators with whom I have initiated projects in which we both did equal work have taken full credit once these were completed. But to me, so long as the work helps the people it's intended to reach, I could care less about whether I get credit or not.

The financial auditing work I was doing put me through col-lege and allowed me to buy my own house in my twenties and gain financial independence. I also continued to volunteer at organizations across New Jersey, like Big Brothers Big Sisters of America (where I'd met Destinee) and Habitat for Humanity, where I helped build housing alongside volunteers and new homeowners, who invest in their future homes or those of other families through sweat equity—the contribution of labor into a project or endeavor. I was a registered volunteer for Jersey Cares, which is an organization that partners with nonprofits, schools, and government agencies and serves as a conduit for residents of the state interested in donating their time. Jersey Cares once paired me with an organization that provides comfort and support to newborns going through drug withdrawal, and I worked as a baby cuddler for a time. These experiences laid the groundwork for my future nonprofit work in Pennsylvania.

After college, I decided to start my own nonprofit addressing food insecurity and education in Newark, focusing on Destinee's neighborhood. It was called More Greens, and I set it up to help teach people who lived on food stamps how to eat well with limited resources. I believed that health and nutrition should be available to anyone and didn't want to be a nutritionist whose services only a few people could afford.

The importance of this work was made crystal clear to me as I began to connect with clients. One of the people I worked with was a mother with three small children. She was a wonderful mom who loved her kids and wanted the best for them but lacked the training and opportunity to provide that. When I met her and visited her home, I noticed that there was no fresh fruit available for the kids to eat. Most of what she had available were processed foods and drinks mostly made of high-fructose corn syrup. As we talked, it was clear that she, like so many others, had never encountered information on the dangers of these sorts of foods in excess or about the importance of integrating fresh foods into her and her kids' diets. When I asked her how she integrated fruits and veggies into their diet, for instance, she noted ketchup as a source because it included tomatoes.

I did not fault her for not knowing more about nutrition. This is not information that we are often taught in school, and without further support, this would have remained a blind spot for her. I connected her with a program that provided fresh produce and cooking classes free of charge. Participating in the program changed the quality of the food she cooked for herself and her children, and she was grateful. I showed her how to read labels and how to choose healthier options for her family, and over the following months, I saw the kids start to get appropriate servings of fruits and vegetables.

Someone asked me once, what gave you the nerve, the courage, to start your own nonprofit at the age of twenty-two? I don't think it is a matter of bravery. Whenever I see a need, something lacking in a community, if it is within my capacity to fill, it feels natural to try to address it. Before starting my nonprofit, I did research to make sure there was not already an organization out there doing the work I ventured to do. At the time, I did not find one working in the community I wanted to serve. There were other nutritionists in Newark, of course, but it seemed like a gatekept profession, one that few I encountered even knew existed, let alone how to access. So I decided to open the door for those who did not know to look for it.

Often, people—especially but not exclusively young people—are held back from pursuing their ideas or trying something new by a fear of failure. *What if I fall? What if no one wants to work with me? What if I don't do a good-enough job?* We subject ourselves to exacting standards even before we start. But I went into the work with no expectation except to do what I could, as best I could. A fear of failure did not register for me, because my goal was not to scale my nonprofit or gain any status from it. I was not looking for recognition. I genuinely wanted to help my neighbors, and their assessment of my work was the only one that mattered to me. As such, the only way I could fail was by not trying at all. It did not matter whether I had one client or one hundred clients. For me, it was simple: The thought of food deserts, that people would be denied such a basic need, kept me up at night. And I believe we should all try to fix whatever keeps us up at night.

There Are No Coincidences

Though providing accessible nutritional education was my passion, I also took on private nutrition clients to subsidize the work I was doing through my nonprofit. Financial auditing was also a well-paid, consistent stream of income, so I continued doing it as a freelancer to pay my mortgage. As a freelancer, I was lucky to be able to operate outside of traditional work environments, which insulated me from the bad behavior I had come to detest. And it was gratifying to do work guided by my own values. I had choice at a time in my life when many are stuck.

Perhaps because my childhood was defined by movement and change, I have never been good at sitting still. I sought out adventure whenever I could—bungee jumping, zip-lining, sky-diving, solo travel—which is how I landed in Costa Rica for a weeklong yoga retreat in the summer of 2007. (I was a committed yogi back then; now, not so much.) To pass the time in the reception area while waiting for class to start, I picked up a copy of *ReadyMade*, a now defunct magazine that focused on do-it-yourself projects. (It was the only magazine available in English and stood out to me.)

Inside was an article on John Fetterman, then the mayor of Braddock, Pennsylvania, who was working to revitalize the abandoned industrial town. Braddock had seen its population plummet by more than 90 percent since its heyday in the 1920s. The town is home to steel magnate Andrew Carnegie's first steel factory—which today boasts one of the few remaining blast furnaces in the region—and free library, and Braddock Avenue was once a vibrant destination for shopping and restaurant-goers. By the 1970s, the booming steel industry had collapsed, and swaths of people and businesses fled. The article described John's amazing political journey and his vision for revitalizing Braddock. He had moved to Braddock to run a GED program, believing firmly in education as the most effective path out of poverty. After two of his students were killed by gun violence, he decided to run for mayor. He won by one vote, beating the incumbent despite not having any previous political experience. John hoped to make Braddock a hub for experimental urbanism, emphasizing communal responsibility and the arts. "Destruction breeds creation; create amidst destruction," he told *ReadyMade* at the time. "Let's insert art into Braddock and see what happens." I remember being impressed by his commitment to his community and the effort to renew and reinvigorate a place he clearly loved that had been all but forgotten.

After I read the article, I set the magazine down and, as I recall, went on to enjoy my time away from home and take in all that the retreat had to offer. But something about that town and its spirited, determined mayor stuck with me. The idea of investing and loving and believing in a place that others had deemed hopeless aligned with my worldview, one that had been clarified by Mr. Rogers: that everyone is special and deserves a chance. That no one place or person is disposable. The way the article described Braddock and the effort that was going into revitalizing it felt like a testament to what was possible if we refused to give up on people and made a deliberate choice to take care of the spaces we inhabit. If we offered everyone the dignity they deserve. John's and the community's efforts were an example of what it meant to pour care into and be responsible for our surroundings.

The article described an old furniture warehouse that had been converted into free studio space for photographers and painters. The church hosted art events and all-night dances to attract partygoers to the town. "For DIY-ers, this town is a dream," John told the reporter. There was so much to be done. But while some may have viewed this as a burden, John seemed to view it as an opportunity, seeing beyond the town's blight and recognizing its potential. It really did sound like a dream.

Shortly thereafter, when I was back home in New Jersey, I read another article that made a brief mention of the fact that some of the steel in the Brooklyn Bridge had come from a place called Braddock. My curiosity was once again piqued. *Braddock . . .* , I thought. *Why does that name sound so familiar?* I remembered the article I'd read, and I took it as a sign that I needed to visit this place. Honestly, I don't know why I felt so drawn to a small city that was six hours away from my home in Newark. I knew very little about Pennsylvania, but that Braddock's name made it to me not once but twice seemed like a sign. Something was pulling me there. I sent a handwritten letter to the borough of Braddock expressing interest in their community and sharing my own nonprofit work. (This may seem old-fashioned and quaint today, but I had grown up on letters, not emails, and I still like the more personal feel of putting pen to paper! I fear letter writing is a dying art.)

I was hoping that someone might be able to serve as my guide, show me around, and tell me Braddock's story. As I read more about this former industrial town, I saw parallels to my own warm but historically ignored neighborhood in Newark. At first glance the two areas might seem like they couldn't be more different, but the closer I looked the more I saw the commonalities. Both places were filled with people who cared deeply for their families and the people around them. Both places were struggling in the face of big economic forces that were out of their residents' control. And both were still working hard to maintain a sense of community and unity in the midst of challenging societal shifts. I felt a kinship to Braddock, and I wanted to contribute to the community there somehow. What form that would take, I wasn't sure. Could I offer to run a summer camp? Could I replicate More Greens there? Was there some other service I could provide that might be useful?

To my surprise, my letter ended up on John's desk. (The mayor probably would *not* personally answer a letter in a big city like Newark!) But John couldn't have been nicer. He personally responded to my letter and said he would be happy to have me visit. I did not know it then, but it was apparently not unusual for folks or media to visit Braddock in those days, when the town was getting a wave of attention in the news. And since the population of Braddock was so small, there was less political bureaucracy, and as mayor, John was often personally involved in any outward-facing commitments.

It took several months of back and forth to find a time that worked for both of us, but that October, I finally drove out to Braddock, relying on a printed sheet of MapQuest directions to guide my way. (I'm aging myself—but Google Maps had only been launched a couple of years earlier and was not yet widely used or available as an application, so getting around was not as easy as it is now.) On the way there, I got lost and pulled into a gas station on Route 30, about three miles away from my destination, to make sure I was on the right path. When I told the man behind the counter where I was going, he looked me up and down and said, "Are you sure? You don't want to go there." For a second, I remember thinking to myself, *Where am I heading?* But I had lived in many places that were perceived to be dangerous or undesirable to outsiders and knew that these were often places with a lot to offer. I couldn't imagine anywhere that I went scaring me.

When I arrived, Braddock was quiet and bright. It was the perfect fall day: The leaves were turning to a golden yellow hue, the sun was low and bright, and the air was crisp. As John showed me around, I was struck first by how, well, *empty* it was. I had lived and worked my entire life in overpopulated urban areas, so I had never been faced with a place that had been so thoroughly abandoned. Once home to more than 20,000 people, the population of Braddock had dwindled to just around 2,700 by then. Homes sat empty except for small relics left strewn across the floor inside (or even on front lawns), like toys, clothes, and even once-cherished photo albums. These were pieces of people's lives, but the people themselves were largely gone. I thought back to my family's emigration from Brazil, when I'd hurriedly packed only the essentials and left the rest of my life behind.

I couldn't stop wondering about the people who had left. Where had they gone, and what were they doing now? Did they still miss their lives in Braddock? I also wondered what it must feel like for the people who stayed behind in Braddock, suddenly surrounded by empty blocks. What was remaining for them here? How did it feel to hold on to a place you loved even after it transformed into something different? How could good people like John Fetterman and other residents rebuild a town that felt hollowed out?

My first impression of John was that he was really tall, towering over me at six foot nine. (I'm five foot nine, for reference.)

My trip was centered on meeting the town rather than him—I loved that Braddock was getting a second chance, and my curiosity had little to do with who was doing the work and more to do with Braddock as proof of the idea that things *could* improve for a community with added focus and attention—so at first I kept my eyes set on taking in my surroundings. But as we kept talking, he struck me as an interesting guy. He was shy, not a big talker except when discussing his work in Braddock, which made him animated and excited. On the day I visited, there was a theater performance at the library and then a reception at his home. I learned it was not unusual for him to host events there. This was part of his approach for drawing residents closer and attracting newcomers to the town. I liked that about him.

John struck me as a good person who really cared about Braddock, and after my visit, we stayed in touch—through phone calls and texts. We talked more about the commonalities between our two hometowns, and about our worldviews, as well. Like me, he did not like to give up on people and approached life from a lens of restoration and compassion. I was impressed by his humanity and how diligent he was in giving people second chances and helping to set them on the right track. He memorized and could recite the GED test results for hundreds of students he had taught. Imagine the love and attention of memorizing and celebrating all those kids' GED scores. So tender. It was clear that many young people looked up to him. He was an example, to me, of leadership from a place of tenderness—inclusive, giving, and equitable. Believing in someone and supporting their path to be the best version of themselves is tenderness in action.

Soon after my trip to Braddock, I invited John to visit me in New Jersey to get to know my city and the work I was doing there. We walked around my neighborhood and in the nearby park, talking about the dreams and hopes we had for our cities and those who lived in them. I took him to where my Little Sister (who is real family now) Destinee, now twenty-six years old, lived in South Newark. And we shared a meal at my favorite Ethiopian restaurant in Montclair. Somehow, we never stopped finding things to talk about.

The next time John and I saw each other was on Thanksgiving, when he invited me to his family's home, which is midway between Braddock and New Jersey. I had already met his parents on the same day I met him—they just happened to be visiting—so it did not feel awkward to spend the holiday with them. They were lovely and welcoming, and our time together felt natural and comfortable. John showed me around where he grew up, and the day after Thanksgiving, we went to the Christmas tree farm and his parents picked out a fir that went up in their living room. It felt straight out of a movie. By the end of my visit, we both sensed that there could be more to our connection and that it was important to pursue it.

One day during my Thanksgiving visit, his mom put pound cake out on the counter. I love pound cake, but I only like the denser, crisper top part. Instead of cutting a wedge of the cake vertically, I sliced the top layer off horizontally and put it on the plate.

John saw what I'd done and immediately teased me. "Did you really just take the entire *top* of the pound cake?" he asked me, incredulously.

His mother jumped in to defend me, saying, "That's the best part!" We all burst into laughter. I don't think I could have done that if I hadn't felt so completely comfortable around them. We laughed a lot that weekend. My sweet tooth and love for the crunchy top of the pound cake is now well-known in the family, and this memory is still the subject of laughter!

He and I were different in many ways. While John was raised by two teenage parents who struggled but eventually became owners of a successful business, my family was still working class. We came from two different parts of the world. He had been raised by two parents, while I came from a multigenerational household and was raised by two women. But despite our different lives and upbringings and family structures, we found we had a lot in common, particularly our shared commitment to service work. (He was also a Big Brother.) We spoke and texted regularly and took turns visiting each other over the next several months. Each visit revealed a new point of connection.

On a subsequent trip to New Jersey, he was walking around my apartment when a book on my shelf caught his eye. It was *Mean Genes* by Terry Burnham and Jay Phelan, which delves into the connection between our genes and our behavior. I was particularly interested in the sections that explained why people make decisions they *know* to be detrimental to their health. As Burnham and Phelan say, "Like it or not, we are each engaged in a battle against our own set of mean genes . . . Masters of the visceral, they control through satisfaction, pain, and pleasure." Though our brains usually win out in this battle, the book teaches us how to walk "the path of most resistance," in which, the writers argue, "we take charge, calling our own shots." Their insights helped me with supporting my nutritional coaching clients, many of whom knew they should be making different choices with their food but just couldn't seem to break out of patterns that weren't serving their best interests. The authors approached the subject with grace and forgiveness and did not shame readers for their choices—instead, they shared their own stories and those of celebrities and other well-known figures to show that the struggle to have self-control, whether it comes to food, money, or other areas, is universal. Burnham and Phelan help readers understand *why* change is so hard. And they share strategies and tricks for how to manipulate your environment to support your goal.

John picked up the book and laughed. When I asked him why, he turned to the end of the book and showed me the acknowledgments. There, the authors had written, "John Fetterman has read and critiqued every chapter (some of them several times)." What? It turns out one of the authors, Terry Burnham, was John's college roommate. Somehow, our connection seemed fated.

As our relationship progressed, I visited Braddock a few more times over the next several months. I was falling for John, of course. But the town, too, kept bringing me back. The more time I spent in Braddock, the more it felt like home. I was drawn to the people, who I viewed as resilient, welcoming, and kind. I also found the Western Pennsylvania landscape to be beautiful in a wild, overgrown way. The topography was intense and striking, full of hills lined with hastily built small homes that once housed the immigrant workers who flooded the town when it was still at the center of steel production. (When friends would come to visit later, I would joke, "Doesn't it look like Aspen?" to which they would immediately respond, "No, Gisele." But that's what I saw in the depth of the mountains around me.) New Jersey, on the other hand? So flat.

I also loved the mix of industrialism and urbanism—seeing children playing, with the steam coming from the mill in the background, felt very cinematic. In May 2008, ten months after we first connected, I took the leap. I made an offer on an empty property in Braddock, even working with a local architect to draw up renovation plans. I love a project and, based on my work on my house in Newark, I wasn't afraid to get my hands dirty with some reno work.

But shortly before I was set to move, the seller changed their mind and the sale fell through. Which is how I found myself moving into John's bachelor pad in the back of an old furniture warehouse in June 2008. One day, when my last box was unpacked, he looked over to me and said, "Gisele, we need to talk."

"What's up?" I asked, still putting away the last of my belongings.

"I don't know if this is working out," John said. I was getting ready to give him a death stare when he burst out laughing. He sat me down and said, "Gisele, I love you so much," and showed me the ring in his hand. He told me its story—he had designed it himself using a vintage stone his parents had bought at an estate sale when he was eight.

"Will you marry me?" he said to me. I excitedly agreed, glad that he had opted for a funny proposal rather than an overly cheesy one. A month later, we went on a road trip to Burlington, Vermont, and eloped. Neither of us planned to get married on that trip. But we did know that we both hated the idea of a big wedding where we would be the center of attention. Maybe that's the downside of my overly tender approach to life—those Big Feelings are often right at the surface, and I wasn't sure I (or my makeup) could handle my emotions and hold back the tears for a full day when I'd be in the spotlight. I also could not bear the idea of inconveniencing other people by making them take time off work or spend money to travel.

Vermont was beautiful and green in the summer sun, and perhaps the romance and magic of the scenery also inspired us to do something daring. One day we just saw a phone book and said, "Maybe we should find a justice of the peace." It was all very quick and reflected how I made most decisions in my life—spontaneously and on a whim. I believe it's important to take advantage of moments as they come. There is so much about our lives that we eventually forget; entire years pass us by and collapse into a few sentences. But every moment we make special we carry with us. All we have are those moments.

Listening to Our Own Inner Voice

We often forget the bravery and curiosity we possess before the counterprogramming sets in. One of my favorite books, *The Little Prince* by Antoine de Saint-Exupéry, explores this loss through the story of an adult who meets a young prince from another planet. Saint-Exupéry dedicates his book to one of his friends, but before doing so, he asks young readers' forgiveness for "dedicating this book to a grown-up." He lists a few reasons for doing so before concluding, "If all these reasons are not enough, I will dedicate the book to the child from whom this grown-up grew." He adds, "All grown-ups were once children—although few of them remember it." It is an apt introduction to a story that is, at its core, about the deficiency in adults' imagination. The dedication positions children as the authority, the ones who know better compared to adults, who have outgrown the important values innate in children.

In *The Little Prince*, the adult is a pilot who meets the otherworldly prince when he crashes in the Sahara Desert. On his planet, of which he is the only inhabitant, the prince cares for a beloved flower and passes the time by sweeping out volcanoes a fraction of his size and walking around the small planet to watch the sunset forty-four times over the course of a day. Eventually, the young prince decides to leave his planet and set off for new worlds. He begins planet hopping, encountering a series of grown-ups on their own solitary planets: a king more concerned with being in charge than being reasonable, a businessman preoccupied with counting and owning the stars rather than admiring their beauty, a vain man who viewed everyone as an admirer. On most stops, the prince came to the same conclusion: "The grown-ups are very strange."

Throughout, the prince laments the daftness of adults, and the narrator adds numbers and facts to appease adult readers, who the narrator says would not be content with a simple story about friendship. "When you tell them that you have made a new friend, they never ask you any questions about essential matters," Saint-Exupéry writes. "They never say to you, 'What does his voice sound like? What games does he love best? Does he collect butterflies?'" Instead, they ask about the prince's age, how much money his father makes, or about his siblings. This is the only way they can validate the prince's existence. It is not enough to hear about the plane-wrecked adult's fond memories; adults must have proof and evidence. "One must not hold it against them," the narrator says. "Children should always show great forbearance toward grown-up people."

Indeed, the transition from childhood to adulthood can be jarring. Say goodbye to imagination, wonder, or gentleness. Say goodbye to effusive expression of emotion or pain. The world of adulthood is concerned with things that are *serious*, like "bridge, and golf, and politics, and neckties." Budgets and 401(k)s and overtime and networking. But the message I took away from *The Little Prince* is that *feelings* are of the utmost importance, as is maintaining a sense of wonder and adventure.

Recognizing the significance of listening to our feelings and intuition has been a big part of my journey of radical tenderness.

Growing up as a tender soul, it's easy to lose trust in yourself. We get good at listening to negative voices that work overtime to drown out the good. Much of what we learn growing up is to seek safety and security. To stay within our expected path and not stray from what we know. But how boring is that? And what guarantee do we have that doing so will truly give us the life we desire?

In a commencement speech to Maharishi University of Management in 2014, the comedian Jim Carrey shared that he believed his father could have been a comic but made a conservative choice rather than pursuing his dreams, opting for a career as an accountant. But that sense of safety was shattered when he was laid off. What witnessing this taught Carrey is that "you can fail at something you don't want, so you might as well take a chance doing what you love." The entire speech is profound and worth listening to in its entirety, but what I took from it is that it's important to listen to your deepest desires—to honor what your inner voice is telling you, and to make space for it to be heard.

To achieve that, we first have to learn to listen to that voice. The voice that gets us excited, that encourages us, that can be impulsive and sensitive. It may sound simple, but how often do we really think about how we *actually* feel as opposed to how we are expected to feel? And how often do we really let those feelings guide our actions? Honing our connection with our inner voice takes practice, because often we are taught that what we naturally gravitate toward or want to do or say to people needs to be filtered through the lens of acceptability. It's why the word "no" is so hard for many, especially women, to say. We do not want to disappoint or fall short of the standard society has set for us. But often, what we are choosing to do is disappoint ourselves to avoid disappointing others. The former is much more painful and difficult to bear in the long term.

The better we get at listening to and discerning the messages that our bodies and mind send us, the more likely we are to live a fulfilling life. Whatever answers we desire already exist inside us. For me, listening to my intuition meant being guided by curiosity rather than fear. I embrace the fact that, no matter how much we plan, the future is uncertain for all of us. And what remains, what I continue to believe is important, are my relationships with and contributions toward other people. So long as I keep these values near, any choice I make will be the right choice. No matter where I am or what I'm doing, I return to my vision for the tender world I would like to see. That pursuit and my intuition guided me from Newark, to that yoga retreat in Costa Rica, to Braddock; it guides me in my career and my life in the public sphere; it guides my interactions with others. The more I listen to my inner voice, the better I get at hearing it.

The goal is not to live a perfect life devoid of mistakes or missteps but rather one that feels fulfilling, rich, and free. Neglecting these values has only ever brought me despair. Because there is nothing more heartbreaking than betraying yourself, even when doing so feels like the easier choice. We are all worthy and deserving of joy, and it is our duty to pursue experiences that bring it forth. Bread and flowers: We need both.

The Little Prince has been a guiding compass, because it gets at the root of what's important in life and what it takes to live joyfully: laughing together, friendships, giving care, and fostering connection. It teaches us how important it is to nurture ourselves and others. These are lessons and attributes children easily grasp, but we lose so much of that magic when we become adults. We lose, or are robbed of, our ability to give tenderness easily and generously. I often wonder what it would look like to reclaim some of that gentleness as adults. Moving through the world, I was like the little prince, appalled at what I witnessed among adults. But I decided, instead, to approach people with curiosity and an open, loving, tender perspective.

Not that this is always easy! Recently, before visiting a food pantry, an acquaintance gave me a heads-up that the receptionist tended to be prickly. "She's a hedgehog," was her exact warning, I believe. We all know people like that—on edge, grumpy, ready to snap. They can really scare us tender souls, who want to avoid conflict at all costs. But instead of shying away from interacting with so-called difficult people, my approach is to disarm them with love. I chose to set aside everything I knew or had heard about her, and instead pretend I was meeting her with a clean slate. We are all brand-new versions of ourselves every day, and I do not hold people to who they might have been yesterday. I give myself and everyone else the opportunity to start their day anew.

"How are you today?" I asked the receptionist warmly as soon as I approached her desk.

"Fine," she responded.

"What did you do this weekend?" I asked. She grumbled a

response. We went back and forth a few more times before, finally, she met my eye.

In just a few short minutes, she completely transformed. I am not sure anyone had engaged with her in that way for longer than a minute in quite some time—asking her about her life, how her day was going, what had been challenging. She was burned out from working with difficult populations in severe pain—like people suffering from mental health issues or unhoused individuals—and the job had become emotionally taxing. Soon, we were swapping stories—she shared that her adult son was struggling with addiction and that he was the source of much of the stress she was carrying around. I realized that her perceived prickliness was a symptom rather than an inherent part of her personality. She dealt all day with people who were coming into the space in some of their worst moments, people who were not always kind to her. Of course she was burnt out, defensive, and reserved.

Hedgehogs' defensive quills point outward when they are feeling nervous or unsafe; it's a way to ward off predators and protect their soft, tender underside. But even these animals can let their guard down once they are relaxed and comfortable. The same goes for us. Part of listening to our own tender intuition is knowing when to engage and press forward—even when it feels scary or awkward.

It's a lesson that I would keep in mind often in the years that followed.

CHAPTER 4

THE POWER OF COMMUNITY

As I built my social circle in Braddock, I embraced the lessons I had learned from *The Little Prince*. The nervous anticipation of moving to a new place soon gave way to curiosity, which opened the door to community and friendship.

Many people tend to tiptoe around new people and spaces, viewing new neighbors with suspicion. This is evidenced all over the country, with the derision of immigrants, the distrust of people with opposing political views, and the everyday altercations caused by casual disagreements. It's natural to be guarded around those we don't know or understand, but it also shuts down any potential for connection. I knew that if I wanted to be happy in Braddock (or anywhere), I needed to be open to the possibility that I could find my people there, just as I had in other spaces.

Rather than approach Braddock with caution, I approached

it with awe. The experience was exciting, I told myself, just as my mother had framed our move to the United States. Walking around the town in those early days, I was a sponge absorbing new information about the town and my neighbors. I learned more about Braddock's deep history. The town is home to the first Carnegie library in the country, built in 1888. I started visiting the Braddock Carnegie Library frequently and attended events hosted there. I learned that Andrew Carnegie was a self-made steel tycoon turned philanthropist who, in the late nineteenth century, gave away hundreds of millions of dollars (the equivalent of billions today). With this money, he founded thousands of public libraries and endowed organizations dedicated to science, education, and other social causes, such as Carnegie Mellon University and the Carnegie Foundation. Carnegie, born in Scotland in 1835, emigrated to present-day Pittsburgh—which shares a county with and is only a short drive from Braddock—with his family as a child. He immediately started working in a cotton factory, working his way up and eventually making a fortune investing in the railroad and steel industries. His first steel mill was opened in Braddock, and it's across the street from where I now live.

At every opportunity in my new home, I talked to people: teen moms, septuagenarian townies, and random pedestrians. I have always been fascinated by people, regardless of their stories, which allowed me to always approach them from a place of curiosity rather than judgment. People often try to change each other in friendships and relationships. But I did not engage with anyone trying to change minds, instead accepting and meeting people where they were—challenging myself to love people into the best version of themselves.

With this mindset, I was able to meet people who would become core parts of my life. Those who would become my friends in Braddock were a little different from the people I knew back home, most of whom were my age. One of my first friends, Ms. Phyllis, is an opinionated now eighty-something-year-old Braddock native who I met at a council meeting. The first time I met her, I learned that she and John were very close, and she peppered me with questions about how I ended up in Braddock and how I had met her "grandson" John.

I recognized in Ms. Phyllis's life some of my own experiences—for one thing, family is everything for both of us, and that includes a shared intergenerational approach to child-rearing. I was, of course, raised by both my mom and my dear grandmother, and Bibi was in turn cared for by Mom when she grew older. Ms. Phyllis engaged in the same sort of intergenerational care, tending to her elderly mother, Willa, for years in her home, until her death in 2021 at 101 years old. And though Ms. Phyllis lives independently, her children are close by and she is able to see them often. She remains one of my favorite people and a close friend.

She is also an example of someone who thoroughly loves, embraces, and cares for her community. One day, I received a call from her. "I'm at the McDonald's on Penn and there's something weird happening," she said.

"What's going on?" I asked.

"There's an older guy. He's with this young girl and she can't look him in the face. He's making her walk behind him. I'm really worried about her." She said the girl had her head down, and anytime she tried to raise it to ask a question, the older guy ordered her to look back down. It wasn't clear what was going on, but Ms. Phyllis knew from the girl's body language that something was wrong. Ms. Phyllis had no formal training in trafficking signs, but she cared so much about people and was always paying attention.

I made some calls and eventually got an organization that works with sex trafficking victims to send help. They were able to save that victim, and later found several other girls who had been harmed by that same man. Ms. Phyllis knows our town, she pays attention, and she speaks up when something doesn't seem right. People like her are an invaluable part of the fabric of any community. I have learned so much from her, and I call her my "Braddock Grandma."

There is almost always a point of connection when you meet someone new, even if your politics are different, even if you were born in different countries or worship gods with different names. You just have to be patient and open-minded enough to find it. I don't limit my friendships or connections to people who agree with me in every way. That would be a lonely way to live, and the reality is that you will never find a person who does. I find that I even disagree with myself at times. Instead, I approach everyone I meet as if they are the best person in the world, because we all have the potential to be.

Let People Take Advantage of You

One of the most rewarding ways to build connections is by giving and receiving service and care. I soon realized that a big part of my role in Braddock as the mayor's wife was to be proactively on the lookout for ways to be of service to others. When I heard a concern from a constituent like Ms. Phyllis, I used any resources I could identify to address it. When someone had a question about how to get something done, I'd try to find the answer. This was a lot of work, but it was a great way to meet people in my new home and continue to learn about the city and state.

Another way I found my community: through my growing family. Soon after John and I married, I became pregnant. My firstborn, Karl, was born in February 2009. I had a water birth at home with a midwife. He was the first baby born in Braddock since the closure of Braddock Hospital's maternity ward decades earlier. Much of those early baby years, when I was focused on keeping my new baby fed and safe, are a blur. At first, I didn't even know how to hold him! In all the photos from his first year, it looks like I'm going to drop him. I lived on parenting blogs and read somewhere that talking to kids like adults rather than using baby talk would help them develop a stronger vocabulary. So I spent a lot of time reading to Karl or walking around town identifying things we saw or introducing him to our neighbors. I remember a lot of strangers who would stop to help me or offer words of support if he seemed fussy or if I looked like I was struggling.

Because I was a new mom, I made a lot of other mom friends. My close friends from back home were also starting families, and though we never missed a milestone in one another's lives, the distance that separated us made it so that we couldn't be there for one another when it came to daily challenges. My new friends in Braddock, on the other hand, were in the thick of motherhood with me, and we got to see our kids grow up together.

One day, I went to my friend Kristen's house and immediately asked if there was something I could do. Please, if I'm ever in your house, do not wait on me. Put me to work! I have a hard time sitting still, and I like having a job anywhere I go. Little milestones are important to me; I like to see that something was accomplished, even something small. I love the before and after, and any small improvement gives me a rush of satisfaction. So I desperately wanted Kristen to give me a task, but she wasn't having it. At least at first.

"How can I help?" I kept pressing her. "Is there anything I can do around here to lend you a hand?"

"Nothing, Gisele," Kristen said. But she seemed busy and stressed out, so I kept insisting. For a bit, she kept repeating that she didn't need anything. But eventually, she gave in.

"You're annoying me," she said. "Go clean my daughter's room." And I did. On another occasion, she invited a group of friends over for a backyard fire pit gathering. I again asked for a job. *Can I weed? Can I rake the leaves?* By then she was used to me, so she mentioned that the stone wall around her fire pit had been falling apart. I picked up the flat rocks that surrounded the crumbling structure and rebuilt it, creating a mosaic-like pattern. Now, after years of friendship, she finally understands: Acts of service are my love language.

Often, when people offer help, our automatic response is to say no. I came across a newsletter recently that addressed this subject and how difficult it is for us to receive help. Written by Sophie Lucido Johnson, an author and cartoonist for *The New Yorker*, her Substack newsletter, titled *You Are Doing a Good Enough Job*, is geared toward "people who beat themselves up." I think a lot of us can relate to that!

In April 2024, Lucido Johnson posted a powerful cartoon on Instagram urging people to "Say yes" when someone offers help. She received a massive response to this illustration, to the tune of tens of thousands of likes, and wrote a newsletter on the topic, reflecting on the resonance of the cartoon and the challenges of asking for help. "Part of the problem is that we're raised to think that we should be able to do the complex ballet of helping and being helped without any written-down or talked-about choreography," Lucido Johnson wrote. "There are scripts that lots of us grow up with instructing us about the rules of help; we observe them throughout our lives, even though they're rarely explicitly stated."

Lucido Johnson identifies some of these scripts: *If I have to ask you to help, it's not really helpful*, or *When you offer to help me, I'm supposed to say no*. These old beliefs—often based on old, outdated, or inaccurate information rather than our everyday lives, can get in the way of allowing us to receive the very real offers of help that those in front of us are extending to us. Our society does not encourage us to depend on one another.

"Consider what it would feel like if you truly felt like you could offload some of the weight of your life onto the people you loved," she said. "Consider what it would feel like if you were the person in the position to do the lightening."

Those words really resonated with me. Because as much as I believe that giving help is important and valuable, it is also important to be open to *receiving* support from others. Many (including me) are more comfortable giving than receiving. It can be hard to hear the word "no" if someone cannot accommodate our request. We are afraid that our friendships will become awkward, or that we will take advantage or be taken advantage of in these exchanges of care. But humans are not meant to weather life alone. Practicing the exchange of care can help us build relationships and forge stronger bonds. We must accept kindness.

In my early years in Braddock, these exchanges became particularly important and valuable in my relationship building. It is around this time that I began to care less about the idea of being taken advantage of. It is up to each of us to set boundaries around what we are willing to give, and so long as I was comfortable with how much of my time and energy I was offering to other people, it did not matter what others thought about how I chose to use my time.

Now, when someone tells me that people will take advantage of me, I respond, "You say that like it's a bad thing. It's not a bad thing." The idea of being taken advantage of itself centers on how my actions are perceived rather than how they make me feel. I want people to spend an afternoon with me to say, "I just met the kindest person ever." That is more important to me than whether others think of me as easy. Giving and receiving care became the foundation for my new life in Braddock.

Author Angela Garbes writes powerfully about this with regard to parenting in *Essential Labor: Mothering as Social Change*, about the devaluation of care work in the United States and the importance of viewing raising children as a communal responsibility. Garbes writes about the network of people she relied on to help take care of her two daughters during the pandemic: her mother, the family's babysitter, and two friends whose children she says she came to love in a way she thought she could only feel about her own daughters.

During this time, she writes, her understanding of parenting expanded, and she began to consider "the work of raising children as *mothering*, an action that includes people of all genders and nonparents alike." She argues that children could (and should) have other caring adults besides their parents who are also involved in the work of mothering them. Much of what she does in the book is reject the very American ideal of individualism, emphasizing the need to embrace interdependence and the inherent way in which we are all linked to one another.

Though Garbes is writing about the exchange of care as it relates to raising children, I believe this idea extends beyond caring for children; it's about caring for one another, for our neighbors, for our friends. Indeed, Garbes alludes to this in an interview with NPR, in which she said, referring to the benefits of sharing the load of caregiving:

> *We need to ask for help. We need to offer help. We need to, from the ground up, insist on our interdependence and do as much as we can to shape our communities the way we want to see them. If we are taking care of each other at the individual level and the community level, if we are helping each other feel more dignified and whole, I think that also gives people more energy to then engage in community work, which may lead to organizing work, which may lead to advocacy. I think that when you receive care from other people, you find, actually, that as depleted as you feel, you might have a little extra something to give.*

Though I still struggle with receiving care or help, I have wonderful friends who ask me what I need when I am feeling overwhelmed. My mother is a lifeline who helps me get through my days. I feel lucky to have her so close. She has been the village in my life, helping both with my kids as well as our furry family members. And I think there is value, too, in freely offering support—giving what is within your capacity while respecting your boundaries. I give without the expectation that others will do the same in return, without holding an imaginary IOU over anyone's head. To me, that is the purest form of giving.

In addition to the friendships and connections I was fostering through daily interactions, being John's wife continued to place me in a position in which people sought me out for help. The population of Braddock was small enough that people often went to John directly with their issues. That means that if a crime was committed or if someone wanted to request a wellness check, *he* was often called instead of or in addition to the police. And if they couldn't reach John, they would come to me. I became the go-to person for residents' concerns and issues, small and large—like a communal emergency contact.

If so-and-so lost a job or had a baby, I was the first to know. Teen moms who were struggling would often drop off their kids for me to babysit or call me if they needed diapers or food from Walmart. After the University of Pittsburgh Medical Center closed the town's only hospital in January 2010, I drove countless people to the hospitals in McKeesport and Pittsburgh. (Access to medical attention in town would remain challenging for five years, until 2015, when John and community organizers managed to convince a competitor to open an urgent care center locally.)

Once, a young mom who was going through a hard time brought her baby over to my house and asked me to watch him for a few hours. I happily agreed. But then, as nighttime fell and there was no sign of her, I became concerned. When I called her, she did not answer. And as one day turned to two, I began panicking, wondering what I would do if she did not come back at all. Karl was less than a year old at the time, so it was hard to juggle two babies as a new mom. She would not come back to pick up the baby for a few days. And when she turned up, tired and out of breath, I took one look at her and decided then not to press her for details about what had happened.

"Are you OK? I was really worried," I said. I knew the broad strokes of what was happening in her life—she was a teen mom who had a difficult relationship with the baby's father and came from an abusive home. She struggled with housing insecurity, often having to couch surf in friends' and relatives' homes. But I did not know what crisis or combination of crises had kept her away that time. She was apologetic and grateful as she took the baby from my arms. And I told her I would be happy to help in the future but would appreciate the contact information for a relative of hers I could reach out to if need be.

Though it was a jarring experience (and I certainly wish she had given me a heads-up), I knew and could empathize with this young mom's predicament. Just one of the things she had gone through could be enough to break someone, but there are many people for whom crises continue to stack up, becoming cycles that are increasingly difficult to break out of no matter how hard they try. Unless you've experienced or witnessed it yourself, it can be hard to fathom the complete lack of support available for so many like this young woman. We assume parents have villages of people available to lend a helping hand. But some don't have many, if anyone, to lean on; they're alone in the world. This can cause extreme distress or exacerbate mental health issues, because these women see no release from the pressures of motherhood. Hers was a symptom of a bigger societal issue. As a society, we needed to do a better job of supporting young moms.

Since then, a crisis nursery called Jeremiah's Place has opened in Pittsburgh, offering free emergency childcare to any family that needs it, no questions asked. I was a board member when it first opened and strongly believe in the work it does. For women like the one I describe above, having a break or the time needed to address pressing issues can be the difference between life and death. It's the sort of service I hope to see replicated widely. Though now, with three kids of my own and a full schedule, it is not sustainable for me to be the go-to person for this sort of drop-off, in those early days I was a bit of a crisis nursery, too.

The more people I talked to, the more committed I became to my new town. I always knew that it was possible to live a good life anywhere, so long as you're willing to invest in it. Many of the people left in Braddock remembered when the streets were full of shops and houses with neighbors. They remember riding their bikes in beautiful, well-maintained parks. And like John and me, they believed the town could be restored.

Together. As a community.

Water the Garden You Can See

Once I settled into motherhood, I got to work getting to know the needs of the community and figuring out what I could get involved in. I started my work in Braddock, as simple as it might sound, with beautification projects. There were certainly a lot of tough issues we were grappling with in our town—poverty, food insecurity, and drug use, to name just a few. I worried at first that my small acts of community restoration might not feel important or significant. But we now know that walking past graffiti and litter on a regular basis can impact people's mental health, and there is a growing body of evidence that shows that environmental conditions can also have an adverse impact on residents' economic and social success.

Art and beauty are crucial aspects of a full life. When our communities are well taken care of, when we can be proud of the spaces we inhabit, it reinforces that we ourselves are deserving of care and instills a sense of self-worth that has tangible effects—one that I believe everyone deserves to experience.

The first thing I did was put up multicolored pinwheels along the town's main avenue. It sounds simple, but the pop of color and seeing them spinning in the wind added a touch of childhood nostalgia to the street that brought people joy as they walked by. I planted flowers, trees, and shrubs, and John and I commissioned and paid for murals. I scoured the town's archives for old imagery of Braddock we could use to honor the town's story. The first one was of a vintage parking sticker that was once used in the town's commercial center. We also uncovered ghost murals—traces of old murals—that we hired talented local artists to restore or recreate. I spearheaded efforts to restore playgrounds and build family-friendly spaces where there were once crumbling structures. I had mock traffic signs made with positive messages. Next to "No parking" or stop signs were others that read "Write more love letters" or "Believe in yourself" or "Eat more vegetables." At the request of a young community member, I added one sign with a microphone that read "Your voice matters." And as the years passed by, I would add other affirmations, too, with residents' input. Drivers would slow down to read and take photos of them. It made me happy that lovely things were being added to someone's day; that an otherwise dull part of boring, everyday life—driving through our town center—had been made more extraordinary and special.

Much of what I accomplished in Braddock at first were small actions. Small acts of service. I had no real plan before I got there, but soon my life began to expand around me. Past the destroyed buildings and empty streets, I encountered the full lives of residents who loved a place enough to continue to choose it even after it was no longer easy to do so. Leaning into openheartedness rather than fear allowed me to construct a new life with people who shared the same unwavering commitment to co-building a community. I decided I was all in when I got to Braddock, and it paid off. It allowed me to access and tend to people's deepest needs, which gave me a medium to affect change. We can't change everything that's wrong with the world, but I believe there is much joy to be found in tending to your own yard. As time went by, it felt like the town was coming alive again.

Eventually, the creative projects took a back seat to more urgent needs. I tried to develop piecemeal solutions to some community concerns. In response to one too many wellness check requests, for example, I collaborated with a youth employment program that John founded to match young people with seniors who live alone. But it was becoming clear that the community needed a more centralized and organized form of support. My second child, Grace, was born in 2011, and with two young kids of my own who I would take with me everywhere, it was becoming more difficult to keep up with residents' individual needs. It was then that I decided to open the Free Store.

On our fourth wedding anniversary, when John asked me what I wanted as a gift, I told him I wanted a shipping container. I had heard somewhere that when shipping containers outlive their utility for transporting goods, many end up in landfills, along with the more than 100 million tons of trash already buried there. Much has improved when it comes to reusing and disposing of them, but at the time, these strong, resilient containers, which were hurricane-proof and made to withstand the elements on the open seas, were viewed as a nuisance. It was a no-brainer to use the opportunity to give one of these containers new life rather than contribute to our environmental contamination. The converted warehouse-turned-loft apartment that John and I shared had a mounted shipping container that served as a second level, which I used as a yoga space, so I knew it could work. I also did not want to deal with the maintenance of having a building—rent, constant repairs, clogged toilets. I wanted my focus to be on the people I would serve rather than the logistics of keeping a building running smoothly. And I wanted the space itself to be a protest, to show what we could do with something that would have otherwise been discarded.

John gifted me the shipping container without asking any questions. Out of it, I fashioned the Free Store 15104, which I envisioned as a one-stop shop that would provide clothing, food, diapers, books, furniture, and other essential items to community members who needed them, free of charge. I placed it in a vacant lot, with permission from the owner, hired local artists to paint its exterior, and installed solar panels. My brother, who is a graphic artist, designed the logo for me. (At the time, I did not know how to use Photoshop, so he often helped me design flyers and other graphics for town events or initiatives. He's still my go-to digital artist and only sometimes complains—but he always still helps in the end.)

Reminiscent of my experiences as a child, much of the inventory at the Free Store is made up of hand-me-downs or discarded items, but over time, we also developed partnerships with stores like IKEA, Banana Republic, Ann Taylor, and more. Outside the shop, I put up a banner that echoed the words Mrs. Barnhill had said to me when I walked into her elementary school class: "Wherever you came from, however you got here, we're so glad to see you." I wanted it to be a place where the most vulnerable people walking through our doors would feel at ease. Just as they had welcomed me, I hoped to do the same for them.

I had done pop-up versions of the Free Store before. When I lived in Newark, a multifamily house on the block where I lived had caught fire, and everyone who lived in it had perished. It had been an entirely preventable tragedy, but the landlord hadn't set up the mandatory fire detectors. After that, I started calling organizations that might be able to donate these lifesaving devices, intent on distributing them to neighbors whose homes lacked this basic protection. It took a few months, but once I'd gathered enough, I put up flyers around the neighborhood advertising the giveaway, and then set up a table on my block where I handed out the fire detectors. The Free Store is an extension of that vision, but it isn't just a place that provides diapers and clothes; it's a catchall for community disasters.

There's real need in Braddock and the Mon Valley, and the Free Store caters to the neediest in our community. That means our team is always dealing with the unexpected. Just recently, a patron had an overdose on our premises. We administered three rounds of Narcan to get them to wake up. They went into cardiac arrest, and I had to give them CPR until the EMTs arrived. People enter the Free Store at their most defenseless, and we have made it into a sort of refuge for anyone who could use a little extra support.

But the amazing thing: There is *so* much support on offer. Many other volunteer organizations in the area struggle to get volunteers and are sometimes forced to shut down because of lack of help. At the Free Store, we don't face these issues. Most of our staff, including Ms. Phyllis, have been with the organization for thirteen years. We joke that someone has to die for us to take on new volunteers. The waiting list to join us had to be capped at one hundred people, and we serve about as many people every hour.

A few years after founding the Free Store, I realized there was an opportunity to address the community's most basic need—food—through simple redistribution. When I was growing up in Queens, my family noticed and lamented that the local Key Food would discard items that did not seem like they needed to be thrown away. Often, the food tossed by grocery stores hasn't gone bad; it's been cleared for new deliveries or because it did not sell, and it was easier to throw it away rather than figure out the logistics of getting it to others who might need it. And I had learned that just one-third of the food discarded in the United States could feed everyone who was hungry.

A food writer and fellow immigrant I had met had the same concern, and we decided to partner to start 412 Food Rescue, a nonprofit that connected grocery stores with organizations or locations that could put the food that would otherwise be discarded to use. We developed an application through which grocery stores like Whole Foods and Trader Joe's could request a driver to pick up produce, desserts, or prepared food and deliver it to food shelters, senior centers, and food banks. The delivery people were all volunteers, and they made their deliveries on bikes, cars, and motorcycles. Often, they got to meet the people they were helping to feed—a personal connection that many told me made the work they were doing feel tangible, essential, real. It showed them what was possible, and it inspired them to think just as boldly.

If you are anything like me, you probably sometimes find yourself overwhelmed or bogged down by all the issues that plague our world. It is tough for me to read about people who are suffering, especially when these social ills feel entirely preventable or fixable. Sometimes, these tragedies hit close to home.

In June 2018, a young man and Pittsburgh native who had been a volunteer at the Free Store was shot and killed by a police officer. He was just seventeen when he died, a goofy kid with a sweet smile, and his death wrecked me. He had started volunteering at the Free Store when he was just thirteen, and after he died we put up a portrait of him, so that we and other community members would continue to honor his memory. Anytime we lose young people so tragically, I struggle to make sense of it, and it makes me wonder if the world will ever get any better. With this young man's death, I felt this more severely. I was acutely aware of all he had to offer to the world, of all he could have achieved, and it hurt me deeply that we had lost him. The officer who shot him was cleared of all counts by a jury the following year.

But I firmly believe the remedy for despair is action. I cannot say for sure that my way is the right way. Sometimes I wonder if my tendency to go, go, go and my ability to adapt to any situation is actually a form of dissociation, perhaps rooted in the uncertainty of my childhood. Whenever I am asked about my future plans, my answer is always the same: "I don't know. I can't see that far." Time is a flat plane that I often struggle to navigate. Details about my past are fuzzy, and it's hard for me to remember when things happened. But even so, this forward momentum has become my way of existing in the world. It orients me when problems feel big and overwhelming. And it has saved me many times over.

Let's be clear: The problems out there are big. The needs in our communities—let alone across the world—can feel crushing at times. And as much as I would sometimes like to, it is not within my capacity to travel to other countries or even other states (at least not regularly) to try to address each community's particular issues. So I focus my efforts on what I can touch, on the people I can reach and see. This sort of localized action can transform our cities and neighborhoods and potentially ricochet into other places, inspiring others to act, too. I regularly meet people who turn tragedy into action, and they are my heroes.

The acts of tenderness and care we engage in daily, whether big or small, can have a profound impact on the people around us. After starting the Free Store, I encountered countless people who offered their time, services, and talents to help my efforts. There is a man who donates handmade quilts to the store. Despite his arthritis, he does the laborious work of creating these beautiful patterned quilts, making more than one hundred every year. I once tweeted about the work he does, and a company that produces arthritis medication gifted him a year's worth of specialty lotion to soothe his joints. There is a woman who spends dozens of hours knitting socks that end up on countless babies' feet. Neither of them ever get to meet the people who are kept warm by the items they donate; they give their time freely and without expecting to be compensated or receive anything in return. These acts create a chain reaction with far-reaching impact.

Before I knew it—because I cared, because I invested, because I sought out and offered help—Braddock had become my home. One day, walking along the town's main road, I noticed a sunflower growing out of the cracks in the concrete. It was on the street near the curb, and I was fascinated by how this flower ended up in this place—a seed carried by a bird or the wind had dropped in this specific spot, and had managed not to be trampled by cars that drove down the street every day. I wanted to protect it. I set up a makeshift barricade, a self-standing white fence, around it to help it grow unhindered.

Eventually, it started curving, like a little umbrella for birds. When it was full-grown, I harvested its seeds and started planting sunflowers around town and in my own garden. These stunning flowers can get so big, their stalk so thick, and it's all from these little, tiny seeds. If you stand in the middle of a field when the sun is going down, you can witness sunflowers moving toward the sun right before your eyes. Each flower head can give you hundreds of seeds. And I've sent what I call "Braddock's World-Famous Sunflowers" all around the country.

Like those seeds, my conversations, run-ins, and collaborations in Braddock flourished into a network that made me intimately attuned to the needs of my neighbors and enmeshed me into the community. We should all aspire to leave things better than the way we found them. Sunflowers do that, improving soil health and attracting butterflies and birds. Be a sunflower to your community.

CHAPTER 5

BARRIERS TO TENDERNESS

I n Braddock, my family and I live in what used to be a car dealership, a wide-open space with extra high ceilings, brick walls, and large ramps previously used to drive in the cars that now lead to the upper floor of our home. The furniture, mostly salvaged from different places in the area—including the steel mill across the street and torn-down churches—is dwarfed by the space, leaving plenty of room for my kids to run around or zoom down the ramps on scooters or rollerblades. It's unusual, it's eclectic, and it's our home. After more than a decade there, I couldn't imagine living any other place.

But it didn't start out feeling quite so comfortable. The building had been vacant for a while when we bought it in 2012. The loft where we had started our marriage suddenly felt too cramped once we began thinking of expanding our family. (My third child, son August, was born in 2014.) We lived in our new home through the renovation, moving from room to room for nine months as the construction crew made its way through the house. It is located across from Edgar Thomson Steel Works, which is home to the only working blast furnace in an area once renowned for its steel production. Looking across the street, I always think of the generations of immigrants who had come there to work since its 1875 opening, and the sacrifices and contributions they made toward the industrialization of the United States. At night, a fifty-foot flame appears that feels like my own personal tea light.

I knew right away that I wanted to make our spacious new home into a place that would be open and available to the entire community. It seemed wasteful not to. Opening up our home to our neighbors seemed like the natural choice in such a tight-knit community, and it proved useful to have a space that allowed for hosting large groups of people.

Over the years (mostly before the 2020 pandemic, while John was mayor), we hosted a slew of events in our home, both personal and community oriented. If my kids had a birthday party, I could invite the whole class. We hosted friends' baby showers, political fundraisers, and many weddings. Before marriage equality was legal, there was a rogue judge who would issue marriage licenses to same-sex couples, and John often officiated these weddings in our home. We hosted Narcan trainings and information sessions for prospective adoptive parents. This has changed since the pandemic, as well as because of security concerns related to John's now larger platform as a senator from Pennsylvania, but for a while, my home acted as a sort of community space for Braddock residents and others who lived in the surrounding area.

One day in March 2015, we planned to host a book event for two local authors. One of the books, *Victim of the System* by Lawrence Fisher, was about Drew Whitley, who had been wrongfully imprisoned for a murder he did not commit. At the event, Whitley told his story of spending seventeen years in prison before Fisher took his case and he was cleared by DNA evidence. The other book, *Striking Gridiron*, by Greg Nichols, was about a local high school football team, the Braddock Tigers, and their efforts to defend a five-season winning streak in 1959 amid a nationwide steelworker strike. It was going to be an inspiring talk with a lot of community support. The event would be catered and open to the public, and many attendees planned to come from surrounding towns to hear these writers read their work.

I spent the day cleaning and clearing the space, making sure our personal items were tucked away and that we were prepared to receive our guests. We hired a caterer who set up in the kitchen with his staff. Slowly, our living room filled with people and the buzz of conversation, as a couple of servers circulated with appetizers and drinks.

Shortly before the reading was set to begin, I slipped past the caterers and into my pantry to hide for a little bit. I love hosting and talking to people, but there were around two hundred guests in our home, and, after a long day, I wanted a moment to myself before engaging with the crowd. I poured myself a glass of wine and checked my phone before walking back out into the kitchen. As I prepared to re-enter the party, wineglass in hand, I felt a tap on my shoulder.

I turned to see an older, immaculately dressed woman with short hair. She leaned in and, lowering her voice, said, "I just want you to know that I saw what you did, and I'm going to tell Mr. Fetterman."

I was briefly confused, and then it hit me: She thought *I* was part of the catering staff, and she believed she'd caught me drinking on the job. I'm not sure why. I was wearing a cocktail dress and heels. I was navigating the space with the comfort of a woman in her own home. Yet for some reason, she looked at me and assumed that, not only was I not a guest at the event, but that I was part of the support staff.

In the past, in uncomfortable situations such as this one, I had always frozen, remained silent, or started to cry. Years before, when I was pregnant with my first child and went to a gala with John, for example, a woman asked me how far along I was. I was seven or eight months into my pregnancy but was carrying small. She was shocked when I shared that I was in my third trimester. Seemingly without thinking how a hormonal pregnant woman might respond to such an inquiry, or that her question might be intrusive, she said, "Oh no. Is the baby OK?" As a first-time mom, I was hurt by the suggestion that I was not taking care of my child, or that there might be something wrong with him. But rather than respond, I burst into tears and stepped to the side. Quite the icebreaker!

But today—several years older and a lot wiser—it was a very

different Gisele the woman was questioning. In fact, she had caught me in the middle of a personal transformation. It had become exhausting to keep having to justify my existence or my life or my family composition. Every time something like this happened and I was forced to explain myself, I felt like I was giving up a little bit of my power. I was left having to deal with both my own pain as well as their shame for misunderstanding. It was frustrating. It was *exhausting*.

Eventually, I realized it wasn't my job to teach anyone or guide them toward understanding me or my family. I didn't want to carry the shame for strangers to whom I did not owe anything, some of whom were operating based on personal biases and stereotypes. I knew it wasn't me to respond with snark or a clapback.

So rather than tell her who I was or that she was a guest in *my* house, I looked at her and said, "Please don't tell Mayor Fetterman. I don't want to get fired!" Then I smiled and walked away. There is nothing wrong with being a server, of course. The work is as important and as valuable as any other job, as is being a babysitter or a housekeeper. But why she assumed that this was my role in that space was a question that was up to *her* to investigate. Frankly, it was not my place to guide her to that answer.

Sure enough, when John and I got up to introduce the speakers, the woman was right in front. We locked eyes, and I saw her face crumple as she recognized me; she was visibly horrified by her mistake. Later, she came up to me. "I really debated leaving," she said. "But Pittsburgh is so small. I know I will see you again." She apologized to me, and I thanked her. Before we said our goodbyes, we shared a toast, and she said, "I'll never make a mistake like that again." It is important to me that people leave every exchange with me with their dignity intact. It was enough for me to simply know that I had neither shamed her nor taken on the labor of educating her.

Learn to Metabolize Anger

I wish I could say that this was the only time I was faced with ignorance or assumptions. Of course, it wasn't. On another occasion, I took my kids to a local pool and sat next to a woman who was also with her three kids. As I often do, I was speaking to my children in Portuguese while lathering them with sunscreen and preparing them to get in the water. The woman turned over with interest and commented that she had tried and failed to find a babysitter who spoke another language.

"That family is so lucky to have you," she said, assuming I was my kids' paid rather than unpaid caretaker.

"I hope they keep me around!" I responded cheerfully. Any woman with kids knows that a child's favorite word is "Mom!" Within a few seconds, my kids were clamoring for my attention, calling me to get their needs met. When the woman realized her mistake, she said, "I don't know why I assumed that." Again, she was left to handle that question on her own.

For me, grace and humor have proven to be the best way to

get through these uncomfortable situations—or at least the only way that works for me. Society or common perceptions of strength would have you think that the best way to respond when you're looked down on or misunderstood is by being confrontational. That by responding in anger, we are teaching people a lesson and letting them know we are not wimps who can be pushed around without consequence.

In part, I get the impulse. In a world that can be hostile toward people like me, anger is a natural and justifiable emotion—even a form of protection. After a while, microaggressions add up and it's hard not to feel frustrated. Some scholars argue that anger can even sometimes be useful. Discussing "healthy anger" in her book *Radical Compassion,* the writer and meditation instructor Tara Brach calls anger "an essential survival emotion."

> *We need to pay attention when it mobilizes our bodies and fills our minds with stories of wrongdoing. It alerts us to marshal our energies against obstacles to our well-being, to create better boundaries, to defend ourselves from physical threats, to make our needs or views heard when we've been silenced. And on a societal level, anger in response to oppression can energize the call for justice.*

As I discussed in chapter two, there are certainly aspects of our society that force us to harden against the world. When facing oppression or injustice, anger can be a tool that intuitively points us toward that which feels unfair or wrong. Though it's not an emotion that has ever come naturally to me, my argument is not that one should never feel indignant or upset. We have a right to be angry when we are hurt.

But anger can only take us so far. As Brach adds, quoting Ruth King, a writer and Buddhist teacher, "Anger is not transformative, it is initiatory." In other words, anger may spur us to action, but it will not necessarily lead us to the correct or healthiest response. To stay in anger, Brach writes, threatens to keep us in a cycle of "chronic blame and resentment" that "hardens into armor around our heart." It pains me to see people walk around with this sort of armor, because ultimately, they end up most harmed.

In their book *Radical Belonging: How to Survive and Thrive in an Unjust World (While Transforming It for the Better)*, Dr. Lindo Bacon addresses how anger can keep us trapped. "If your anger is reactive and unthinking, it protects you from fully feeling the discomfort of the injustice," they write. "If you couple your anger with a recognition of your own value and awareness that the problem is the circumstances, not you, you can use your anger to set boundaries and stand up for yourself." Recognizing that the problem does not lie in me has been transformative and allowed me to let go of the need to prove myself to others who do not see me as fully human. Once I realized, for instance, that being confused for a babysitter or server does not faze me, because I see immense value in those jobs, it became easier for me to approach and leave those interactions feeling whole.

There are moments, of course, that do not allow for grace or humor. One day during the pandemic, I decided to stop by Aldi to buy golden kiwis while they were on sale. Aldi is one of my favorite places—a chance to people-watch and unwind while browsing the aisles. The lines were long, and people were social distancing and wearing masks. While I was waiting, I heard and saw a commotion in my peripheral vision. A visibly agitated woman was yelling obscenities, and at first, I thought, *How sad, what the pandemic is doing to us.* It took me a second to register what she was saying and another to realize that her comments were directed at me. She was calling me a thief and telling me I "don't belong in this country." She said I had "ruined John's bloodline." I was frozen, in shock. The hate and darkness in her face was, frankly, terrifying.

But as I've said, I'm not one to steer toward confrontation. I finished checking out, paid, and left the store; still, the encounter was not over. She followed me out to the parking lot and started yelling racial slurs at me from outside my car. I had never met this woman before. She was a stranger who, for some reason, felt disgust and hatred toward me. I could see it in her eyes.

In that moment, I didn't have the energy to think of something witty to say, nor do I think she deserved any response. I was shaken and in shock and sat sobbing in my car for a long time. I reverted to my childhood self, once again that undocumented little girl who feared being deported. I did not go back to Aldi for months following the incident. (The company reached out to me and banned the woman from all its stores.) I was heartbroken and my sense of safety had been shattered. Not only at being subjected to that sort of vitriol, but that it existed in the world at all. But rather than respond to aggression with aggression, I let myself feel the pain of the moment and left. There is no shame in walking away. Socially, we still place value on being able to tough out difficult situations. Women who are in work environments dominated by men are praised for breaking glass ceilings, and public figures who get harassed are applauded for being able to take it. But nothing is lost when you refuse to engage.

Plenty of people would feel an unequivocal need to verbally defend themselves in that moment. They'd see it as necessary to not allow the abuse of the bully to go unchecked and thus continue. It's just not my way. What would have changed if I had engaged this woman? If I had yelled, or cursed at her, or worse, physically attacked her—after all, she wasn't likely to be chastened by reasonable discourse—would she have become less hateful?

Some argue there is value in making others feel shame. In a column for *The New York Times*, Tressie McMillan Cottom wrote that "despite the bad rap that shame gets in our overly psychoanalyzed culture, it is merely a feedback loop that tells you something about your behavior as well as the expectations of others." Shame or being shamed, she argues, can point others toward correct action or let them know that what they are doing is not socially acceptable.

That may be the case, but I do not believe it is my place to dole out shame, even when it's deserved. It is not my responsibility to take on that labor. Responding to the woman in the parking lot would have only been a betrayal of myself and my own character. I'm reminded of the scene in the movie *You've Got Mail*, in which Meg Ryan's character Kathleen tells off Tom Hanks's Joe Fox, the big box bookstore owner driving her independent shop out of business.

"For the first time in my life, when confronted with a horrible, insensitive person, I knew exactly what I wanted to say and I said it," she told Joe. But later, writing to her online pen pal—who, unbeknownst to her, was also Joe—she admits, "Of course, afterwards, I felt terrible, just as you said I would. I was cruel, and I'm never cruel."

The circumstances are completely different, of course. I doubt this screaming woman and I are swapping stories and consolations in some anonymous online forum. But I think the idea stands. I will not be who I am not for the sake of punishing those who attempt to harm me. I keep myself safe by refusing to let others' actions define me. This allows me space to take care of my own emotional needs and those of my family.

Stand Firm in Yourself

I no longer feel the need to correct people when they make assumptions about me, because their opinion or view does not dictate my inherent value. No one has the power to take respect away from me. No one. Because I have realized and internalized that how other people choose to behave has nothing to do with me.

Once, my daughter told me a story about a friend who had shared a secret widely that she told her in confidence. "I felt so embarrassed," she said.

I told her that no one should be able to make you feel embarrassed. "Why were you embarrassed, honey?" I responded. "You didn't do anything wrong." Often, we internalize other people's actions and words. It makes us question ourselves or rattles our sense of self. It is not that these mean comments or microaggressions do not hurt me—I am a deeply sensitive being, after all, and I cannot help how I feel. But whereas in the past I would feel embarrassed or ashamed when some aspect of my life or my identity was questioned, now I focus on leaving the shame where it belongs. For me, crying, when it does happen, is the moment of silence I use to redirect my thinking. It's when I can ask myself, *What part did I have in this? How much is mine to carry?* It is both a release and a reset—a moment to process what happened and designate appropriate responsibility. Because ultimately, someone else's actions belong to them alone.

I wear my former immigration status on my sleeve, and it often becomes a pain point for others to press. People from all walks of life come into the Free Store, and on one occasion an elderly veteran came in for food. I handed him a premade meal from Costco, and in that moment, I received a call from my mother. We started speaking in Portuguese, and this triggered a verbal attack. The man accused "people like me" of stealing jobs from Americans. He berated me for my mere presence in the country. The irony of the situation was not lost on me. Here

I was, fulfilling this man's need, giving rather than taking, and he could only see me as an intruder.

Often people get triggered by how they're being perceived or treated because, deep down, maybe they believe a piece of it, too.

"Whether we realize it or not, it is our woundedness, or how we cope with it, that dictates much of our behavior, shapes our social habits, and informs our ways of thinking about the world," writes Dr. Gabor Maté, discussing trauma. "It can even determine whether or not we are *capable* of rational thought at all in matters of the greatest importance to our lives." Both how others treat us and the way we respond is defined by our past experiences and the imprints these have left on us. Identifying these patterns is crucial to reclaiming control over our behavior. When others look down on us, it can feel like a confirmation of the voices in our head, like we've been found out. But often, it's the other way around: others directing their insecurity in your direction. When you resolve what has been triggered in you and learn to stand firm in your own sense of self, it's easier to let what others think slide off your back—and to extend compassion to others.

When someone hurts me or attempts to, I do not let it land or stick. It does not linger in my thoughts or in my bones. Doing so would be to internalize fault for behavior for which I am not responsible. It grants people the power to upset me or change the way I view or feel about myself. We need to take back that power. All we have control over is how we choose to respond and let it exist in our bodies.

It's a profound shift in thinking to internalize that no one has power over your own self-perception. When you know in your heart that you are inherently worthy, no one else can shift that. It's freeing to let go of the idea that personal value or validation comes from the outside. So, while I do get sad, the difference is that I get sad for *them*. For the person who has not yet realized the effects of their actions or words. The person whose idea of family and identity is so limited that it does not expand to embrace my complexity.

In our interactions with others, there is always the opportunity for both harm and connection. Though not always intentional, people will try to hurt your feelings or make you angry, and it's natural to want to respond in kind. It's a sort of knee-jerk response to injury: you hurt me, so I want to hurt you back. We think this will make us feel better, or at the very least make others feel worse. But what do we gain by responding with anger or aggression? Especially when the person on the other end does not recognize our full humanity.

In some ways, I'll admit, I adopt a practiced naïveté when it comes to the hatred that I know is out in the world. It feels necessary in the high-visibility space that I occupy and, also, to be able to do my work with an open mind and heart. Toni Morrison once wisely said that racism is a distraction, keeping us on the defense and forcing us to justify our existence over and over. Rather than give in to this inclination, I prefer to put that energy into those who I feel more naturally connected to and who want to relate to me.

Letting People Go

This practiced detachment is, admittedly, harder when the person on the other end is not a stranger. It hits differently when the person who is hurting you is someone you are close to and trust.

During one of my pregnancies, I attended a baby shower for an old coworker. I was excited to see so many friends and to celebrate another woman's journey into motherhood. One of the guests was a close friend who I had worked with for years and who had even asked me to be the godmother of her child. When I got home, there was a message in my inbox. She had sent me, apropos of nothing, a rambling email accusing me of lying about my pregnancy and stuffing my belly with a pillow to fake it. It was clear she was using me as a dumping ground because she knew I was not the type to fight back. "I don't know why you're saying this, but you're wrong," I responded.

Another time, my relationship with a former business partner who I was friendly with soured because of behavior that did not sit right with me and misaligned ideas about how to run and lead the business. In both cases, I opted to walk away from these relationships altogether. Neither was worth my sense of peace.

Often when people harm us or attack our character, we internalize it as a rejection, and it can activate our internalized shame. At another time in my life, I might have internalized what was said to me in the email from my friend and applied it to my self-image, but by then I understood that we just were not meant to have a relationship with each other anymore. Dr. Bacon writes in *Radical Belonging* that rejection "threatens our sense of belonging." They suggest that when we are rejected, whether it's by being broken up with or not being invited to lunch with our colleagues, we can reframe it not as a personal issue but as a mismatch between us and the other people. Perhaps your communication styles don't mix well, or maybe your values are too different. Whatever it might be, it's important to remind yourself that whatever the other person is seeing in you that they do not like does not define all of who you are. To recover from rejection, writes Dr. Bacon, "you need to remind yourself that you are appreciated and loved" by others, even if there is someone who does not value you.

It can be hard to walk away from difficult, or even abusive, relationships. There is a misguided belief that when you love someone, you must tolerate their misbehavior—a toxic mutation of the idea of unconditional love. But this is a misunderstanding of what love is. In bell hooks's manifesto on the value and importance of love, she argues that few know what love is or have ever experienced it. The reason for this is that we have been taught erroneous definitions of love. Many wrongly believe that love is merely a "good feeling," she writes. But love is, in fact, an *action*. She defines love as a mix of various ingredients, "care, affection, recognition, respect, commitment, and trust, as well as honest and open communication." If someone claims to love you but does not practice the basic tenets of loving, then that is not love at all. Our first commitment, always, is to ourselves.

Only in fully loving ourselves can we learn to accept love from others in a way that is generative, healing, and mutual.

Years later, the friend who wrote me the email apologized and explained that she had been going through a difficult time when she wrote it. It had, as I suspected, nothing to do with me. And that's usually the case in most negative interactions. The exercise I did when I was younger, in which I would concoct backstories for the villains in my life to explain their bad behavior, proved useful and true to real life. Most often, how other people treat you reflects them rather than you. Like Bibi would always tell me, we can only give what we have inside.

Whenever someone attacks or is mean to another person, it usually means they are in pain themselves. The worst people I meet are probably those who are suffering the most. This understanding helps me both separate their bad behavior from myself but also separate *them* from whatever awful thing they have said or done to me. It helps me to humanize them and keep going. I always tell my kids, "You have to love difficult people, because you are also one of them. Someone has probably found us difficult at some point." It's easy to love people who are nice. But I challenge myself to learn ways to love people who are mean and difficult, too. It's an exercise that requires committed practice, and I practice it every day. No one should be remembered for their worst, or even their best, day. We are all learning, growing, and trying to get home.

I once had a Free Store customer who for years was prickly and rude to me. In every interaction, he was dismissive and argumentative. Because he was a patron of the store, and our doors are open to everyone, this was not a person I could walk away from. So I really dug in and committed to either winning him over or figuring out what he was going through. It took *years*, without exaggeration, before he softened. I later learned that he struggled to trust people because most people in his life had let him down. I am happy to have invested the time and patience. People can be amazing—sometimes it just takes a few years.

Unkind words do not come naturally to me. I am the personification of a bleeding heart, a descriptor that has been hurled as an insult toward liberals in recent years but that I wear with pride. My kindness is not a façade, which confuses people. I'm not cursing anyone under my breath or talking about them behind their back. I truly don't have it inside me.

But this practice of disconnecting others' actions from my own feelings helps me move on more quickly from the pain of being misunderstood or harmed. It helps me continue to move with compassion and empathy while reducing harm to myself. I stand firm in the fact that it is not my fault. I set boundaries or walk away rather than engage in a fight. It feels like a waste of my energy to choose a negative interaction in which I will either receive further harm or find myself in the impossible position of trying to change someone else. I would rather use that energy on people whose values are aligned with mine and who do not choose destruction over healing.

When we are our authentic selves, we leave room for people who match our energy to find us. I've always been drawn to people who are vulnerable and kind, and who do not make me feel wrong for my way of being. I have no interest in surrounding myself with people who keep me in a constant state of friction—who make me feel like my gentleness is a bad thing. In the past, I've felt like my sensitivity is something I need to fix or work on, a kink in my armor or a bug in my programming. But now I know I don't want to wear armor. Maintaining my tenderness is my own social boundary and pathway toward attracting the right kind of people for me. And I've realized that it's my strength in all my relationships. Those who don't appreciate it are free to find a better fit for them.

CHAPTER 6

PLEASE CALL ME SLOP

As I was settling into Braddock, John was advancing in his political career. In 2019, he became lieutenant governor of Pennsylvania, which made me its Second Lady. Before becoming one, I had never really heard of that title at a state level, nor did I know what it entailed. All I knew was that as soon as I became Second Lady, something shifted. Suddenly we had security, and people started opening doors for me and calling me ma'am. It was a strange adjustment.

In Braddock, though John was mayor, there never seemed to be a hierarchy. People still called to ask me for favors and spoke with me casually. By that point, I was running around with three little kids, taking them to music and dance classes, running my nonprofits and volunteering—life was very much as it had been for years. I was just one of the local moms. But outside of the community things felt . . . different. Everything suddenly felt much more serious. My attendance was suddenly required in spaces where it hadn't been before. The state troopers had to accompany me and do a safety sweep anywhere I went. And places I had visited before as a volunteer started organizing welcome committees that waited by the door to greet me.

I understood and appreciated that this was meant to be a sign of respect. But as someone who doesn't believe in social stratification, this shift made me uneasy. As a child, seeing my mother talked down to and treated differently in the United States compared to how she had been regarded in Brazil had opened my eyes to these false hierarchies. I'd seen firsthand the ways in which something as circumstantial and irrelevant as a document, a job, or an accent could change the way you were perceived. When my mother asked questions in her accented English, people often raised their voices in response, as if a higher decibel was the key to breaking through the language barrier. It was clear that people made assumptions about her intelligence based on how she sounded, as well as on the caddy of cleaning supplies she often carried around when she had just gotten off or was going to work. To their eyes, these qualities made her somehow less valuable, less deserving of respect.

That I was experiencing the opposite effect did not make it sit any better. I did not want to be treated better; I wanted to continue to be received based on both my inherent value as a human as well as the merits of my contributions—*not* my proximity to my husband. It clashed with one of my core values: Nobody is better than anybody else.

Still, now that I had the title of Second Lady of Pennsylvania, I was determined to use it for good and to mold it to fit *me*, instead of the other way around. From the beginning, I was adamant that my life, as well as the kids', would be separate from John's career. Often, being a politician takes over everything and defines the family—likely because it's viewed as important and dominated by appearances. I respect his work but did not believe it should overshadow our lives. John's new position meant that he had to travel across the state and was often gone for days at a time. We missed him, but I also think distance is healthy in any relationship, and it made us cherish the moments when we were together even more.

The position of lieutenant governor also came with a three-story, 2,400-square-foot stone house located in Fort Indiantown Gap, right outside of the state's capital of Harrisburg, Pennsylvania: the Lieutenant Governor's Residence. We would also have a full staff—a gardener, housekeeper, and private chef. As cushy as it all sounded, it was a no-brainer to turn it down. We didn't want to uproot the kids, and it felt wrong to have the taxpayers foot the bill for us to live in a mansion when we had a perfectly good car-dealership-turned-home back in Braddock. It also felt like an unnecessary luxury and antithetical to how I had grown up. (Though those who know my cooking ability, or lack thereof, know what a sacrifice it was to give up a private chef!) Instead, John rented an apartment right by the Capitol in Harrisburg, where he would stay when he was presiding. I would spend most of my time in Braddock, but I felt a responsibility to figure out what I could do in this new position to help a broader group of people across Pennsylvania.

Becoming Second Lady

Though we did not want to live in the L.G. Residence, I saw an opportunity in the Olympic-sized swimming pool on the property. It felt outrageous that only one family would get to use it. I was also aware of the dark, ugly history of exclusion of Black people from swimming pools.

In nearby Pittsburgh, a group of Black patrons had been beaten by white patrons in 1931 for attempting to access a newly opened public pool. Such episodes continued for decades, despite the state not having any official law prohibiting Black people from swimming in the state's pools. The impacts of this history are still present today, with the fatal drowning rate among Black children nearly three times higher than that of white children. So many kids never get access to swimming lessons or water activities. Given this history, it did not seem fair that only my own children would get to enjoy a pool funded by tax dollars.

We decided to democratize its use and repurpose it as the people's pool, open for summer camps, schools, churches, and nonprofits to reserve. On opening day, students from the Harrisburg School District nervously splashed around in the shallow end. I bought a carful of pool toys and goggles, and we handed out stickers that read "You belong here and everywhere." The kids became weekly visitors to the pool, and by the end of the season, many had passed their swimming tests and made their way to the deep end. Thousands of people came and swam with us through those four years that John was lieutenant governor (except for the year it was closed due to the pandemic), including members of one of the state's first Black churches. We were the first and only second family to turn down living in the mansion, and the state legislature eventually approved its sale to a veterans' organization.

It was still a bit uncomfortable every time someone introduced me as Second Lady of Pennsylvania, but I was glad to be challenging how things had always been done in politics. To make the title more accessible and fun, I took to asking people to call me SLOP for short. For obvious reasons, people warned me that the nickname wasn't flattering. But it amused me, and I put it in my Twitter bio. It became a running joke, and for the next few years, people would mail me custom shirts and other items that said "SLOP." One day, my mom called me upset. "Why are these people saying these horrible things about you being mushy meat?" She had googled what the word meant, and I had to reassure her that I had given myself the nickname.

At times, despite my best efforts, the reality of what it meant to be in politics and the limitations it placed on our lives were unavoidable. In February 2020, for instance, I participated in a Brazilian Carnival event that happens annually in Pittsburgh, a weeklong celebration characterized by a festive parade, lots of dancing, and colorful, bejeweled, and often revealing outfits. It was exciting to participate in an event that highlighted such a joyful aspect of my culture, and I did not think twice when John posted a photo of my costume to his Twitter, showing me in a gold bra-style top with blue and orange gemstones and an exposed midriff. It was a lighthearted post in which he joked that he was going to have the state historian confirm that I would be the first Second Lady to dance at the event. Before long, the tweet had attracted a flurry of responses, and some seemed to criticize me for wearing a skimpy outfit. John immediately jumped in to defend me and blocked a couple of Twitter users. But those two men threatened to sue him, arguing that because Twitter was a "designated public forum" and John an elected official, blocking users was a violation of their First Amendment rights. John was forced to unblock them. Never could I have imagined that my Carnival outfit could lead to a legal crisis. Something that started out lighthearted quickly became a serious political issue.

Still, I did my best to actively push back against the cachet of being Second Lady and tried not to let others' criticism dictate how I lived my life. My focus was on serving residents of the state just as I had those in my community. In addition to running the Free Store, I was taking on statewide campaigns, becoming a census ambassador, and supporting the launch of a program that allowed students to count foreign language instruction toward college credits. But I soon learned that that sort of exposure did not look or feel the same as it did in Braddock.

Now, I found myself meeting people who tried to get close to me to gain access to John. There were some I knew had not been supportive of his campaign, who now approached me after he won and said, "We were on your side from the beginning." People were still calling me when they couldn't reach John, but now the asks were coming from journalists or people who wanted to invite him to events. It was most surprising coming from people who presented themselves as feminists or progressives—people I would expect to understand what it meant to use a woman as a proxy for a man. I wasn't on John's staff, but I was treated like one of his aides. The experience was incredibly draining.

The comments that most grated on me during these times were those that tried to position me as the "good" type of immigrant. People sometimes told me, in what they thought was a compliment, that they would have no problem with immigration if all migrants were like me, or more confusingly, I would sometimes hear that I didn't "look like an undocumented person." They liked me, they said; it was *those* immigrants they could not tolerate. I would usually respond, "I *am* those immigrants." I had no interest in being painted as the model (in other words, palatable) immigrant at the expense of demonizing others who were similarly looking for a better, safer life. I did not want to perpetuate respectability politics, which tell us that if only disenfranchised people behaved a certain way, it would be easier for others to accept or respect them.

Nor did I want to make it acceptable for others to look down on undocumented immigrants. When people made a distinction between me and "other" immigrants, I felt like they could be talking about my mom, or people I love—people who were not married to lieutenant governors but were no less deserving of their respect. Seeing the way my mother was dismissed growing up stayed with me, and I rejected any attempt to draw a line between me and people who were likely suffering. I still see that sort of behavior happening with people today, whether it's because someone has an accent or otherwise looks or sounds like they don't belong. Even at the Free Store, I've seen customers upset by someone they couldn't understand. Witnessing these types of interactions has made me adamant not just about affirming others' value, but also my own. No matter where I am, I belong just as much as the person next to me—even if others do not see it that way.

After any of my political events, I came home and went straight to the Free Store. None of those places feels different to me in terms of importance, and my value does not change either. I have a lot of friends who leave a party or an event and worry about whether people liked them, whether they said the right things—I've never been that person. I've never had imposter syndrome. I know I, like everyone else, have a lot to offer. People should *want* to be around me and around you, too, reader.

I'm reminded of the oft-repeated Zora Neale Hurston quote: "Sometimes, I feel discriminated against, but it does not make me angry. It merely astonishes me. How can any deny themselves the pleasure of my company? It's beyond me." We should all internalize this message. Those who do not accept or see us fully are missing out. It's *their* loss.

The Great Equalizer

A year into John's term, the COVID-19 pandemic gripped the country and the world, and my attention once again returned to

Braddock and my family. I found myself at home with three kids, removed from the in-person activities of being a Second Lady. At a time when the need was greater than ever, we were forced to close the Free Store and shelter in place. If my family, with all its privileges and benefits, was suffering, I could only imagine what others were going through. We were forced to get creative about how we offered aid to community members who, already struggling, were placed in an even tighter bind.

We started by doing porch deliveries of food and baby supplies for local families with young children. Looking around my home and seeing the plethora of toys, electronics, and reading materials available for my kids to entertain themselves, it occurred to me that there were likely families who did not have much to keep their kids busy to distract them from their confinement. We delivered new toys to more than three hundred kids in Braddock and surrounding areas.

During the pandemic, the stress and fear intensified drug use across the country, placing people at a much higher risk for overdose. Families with members who were addicted to substances reached out to ask if we could provide Narcan, which we had for a long time offered at the Free Store. In one case, a woman reached out to tell us her son's life had been saved by the Narcan we delivered. We handed out masks and, once the vaccine was released, I recorded multiple public service announcements in Spanish to encourage Pennsylvania residents to social distance, wear masks, and get vaccinated. We also hosted a weekly pet pantry to give out food for pets. Despite our physical location being closed, we were as busy as we had ever been.

The pandemic proved difficult for someone like me. I'm an extrovert who regularly goes around chatting with and hugging people. Not being able to have those daily chance interactions was a huge loss and shift in my daily life. I saw a meme around that time that read "Check on your extroverted friends because they are not OK." I felt it deeply. I missed connecting with people and exchanging energy. I missed hearing people's stories. One day, I went to Costco and looked up to see that everyone was wearing a mask. It occurred to me that the masks made it impossible to see anyone's smile, and I was hit with a wave of sadness. I ended up crying in the chocolate section. In the next aisle, I heard someone else crying, too.

It was around this time that I was diagnosed with ADHD. I had been going nonstop since the start of the pandemic and was inspired to get tested after my work partner told me, "I love working with you, but your brain is insane. You must have ADHD." After my diagnosis, all my behaviors suddenly made sense to me: my inability to sit still; my tendency to jump from project to project; the ways in which I became easily distracted in conversation by a passing car or a butterfly. I tend to over-schedule myself and fill my days with things to do. I vacillate between two states: completely overwhelmed or dreadfully bored—and I try to avoid the latter at all costs. This became heightened while I was stuck at home, looking for ways to keep both my kids and me busy and constantly thinking up new ways to serve the community. I planted sunflowers in town and re-paved a local street, Maple Way, with abandoned bricks I found on my daily walks. Every day there seemed to be a new community need to fulfill.

Though I missed the consistency of going to the Free Store, I was grateful to be present for more little moments with the kids. In some ways, I felt like I was also connecting with my inner child. One day we went to the park, and I started drawing on the ground with chalk while my kids looked on from the sides. My tween daughter asked, "What are you, ten?"

We flew kites, which reminded me of my childhood in Brazil, where my cousins and I would make our own kites out of bamboo and tissue paper and fly them for hours. I taught the kids to make glass mosaics and wind chimes. We made tie-dye T-shirts and painted stepping stones for our neighbors. We went on daily walks and visited nearby waterfalls and parks. When my son August lost a tooth, he pondered out loud, "I wonder if the tooth fairy is allowed out? Which county does she live in?" We adopted our dog, Levi. I celebrated both my brother and my Bibi's birthdays remotely. Our days were weird and beautiful. Every moment felt precious, made more so by the intense gratitude I felt for having all that we needed to keep us healthy and well.

All families were impacted by COVID-19 to varying degrees, and mine was no exception. I lost my Tio Telmo, the uncle who had been a father figure to me when I lived in Brazil. Tio Telmo was a former intelligence agent who worked for ABIN, the Brazilian version of the CIA. He was my favorite person growing up, always around and on my side, no matter what the situation—a parking ticket, a bad grade, a breakup for which I was to blame. He found a way to make me in the right, often in funny and indefensible ways. And as I got older, when he would visit us in New Jersey, we would go on trips or to the casino together. When I would introduce him to a boyfriend, he would joke, "Oh, but wasn't the guy I met last week a different person?" He loved me unconditionally and thought I hung the moon.

Tio Telmo was intubated and in a coma for nearly a month until he died in June 2020, and every day that he was hospitalized I sent him voice notes and texts that I hoped he would wake up to read. I have a wall of photos in my house, and in the month after he died, his photo kept falling on its own. I would hear a loud thud from elsewhere in the house and when I ran over to the source of the sound, it was always his picture on the floor, as if he was lingering, reminding me that he was still around. When I miss him, I listen to one of the hundreds of old voice notes he sent me on WhatsApp, all of which start with his nickname for me: "Princesa!" Our last messages were an exchange in which I sneakily told him that Bibi, who was in Brazil at the time, wanted Espada mangoes—a yellow, oval-shaped variant of the fruit—but did not want to bother him and ask him to go to the market. I asked him to get them without telling her I had called, and he said, "Of course, I'd never rat out my favorite niece."

As much as I was devastated by the way the virus ravaged communities and my family, I was also inspired by the hometown heroes who stepped up to help. Dozens of people reached out to me to ask how they could support my efforts. An elderly woman who lives in nearby Braddock Hills hand-made hundreds of masks for me to distribute to community members but did not even want the credit.

"Can I put a picture up?" I asked her. "Can I thank you?" But she insisted on being anonymous.

Elsewhere in Pennsylvania, several dozen workers at a factory that produced personal protective equipment volunteered to stay there and isolate from their families to make sure essential workers had what they needed. They ended up staying there for nearly a month. Forty people sacrificed their time with children and loved ones to help protect the health-care workers who were putting their lives on the line to keep us safe. The beauty of that generosity and sacrifice still makes me tear up.

There were countless examples of neighbors helping neighbors, people pulling one another up when we were all going through one of the worst crises of our lifetime. They were an example to me of the inherent goodness that exists in all of us, and the care they provided despite personal sacrifice reaffirmed my faith in humanity. We showed the best of ourselves, and I witnessed so many acts of tenderness, big and small.

Amid all this tragedy, former president Donald Trump attempted to end the Deferred Action for Childhood Arrivals program, which has allowed nearly 535,000 young people who arrived in the country as children to avoid deportation, further their studies, and legally work in the United States. To attack Dreamers at all—but particularly in the middle of a global pandemic—seemed to me the utmost expression of cruelty. Dreamers were among the health-care workers who were laboring tirelessly to curb the impact of the virus. Though the attempt was shut down by the Supreme Court, it reflected to me the way that migrants are consistently devalued in American society. Millions of migrants were essential workers, picking our food, making sure our supermarket shelves were stocked, and working in custodial jobs sanitizing businesses that remained open, often at great personal risk. And yet they were not eligible for the stimulus checks that were a lifeline for families struggling across the country. This felt like a form of punishment for a community that was contributing so much during a vulnerable time. They were deemed unworthy of support simply because they were born somewhere else, like me.

I could not help but think back to my own childhood and what would have happened to my family if a pandemic like the one we experienced had broken out back then. I am not confident we would have survived. My mother became a citizen in the summer of 2020, after thirty-one years in the United States, and it reminded me that our past is not so far away.

The essential contributions of Dreamers and undocumented people during the pandemic reaffirmed their place within the core fabric of our country. As much as the pandemic highlighted and exacerbated inequality, for me it was also a great equalizer. Everyone was touched by its devastation in one way or another. And we learned that we all play a role in keeping our country running and in keeping one another safe. To me, America is not the birthright of people of a particular skin color or class. It belongs to anyone who is willing to work for and invest in its future.

In September 2020, Tom Jawetz, vice president for immigration policy at the Center for American Progress, testified before the U.S. House Judiciary Subcommittee on Immigration and Citizenship urging its members both to take action to further support immigrant workers and also acknowledge their ongoing contributions. "Just as these folks are doing essential work now and have long done essential work, we know their work will be critical going forward, both as we continue to deal with the coronavirus—for who knows how long—and as we take steps to begin to rebuild and strengthen our economy," he said.

Yet as I write this, these contributions seemed to have been quickly forgotten post-pandemic, as immigration continues to be a contested issue leading up to the presidential election—all while Latino voters remain a coveted voting bloc. There continues to be a lack of compassion toward immigrants, both those who live in the country already and those seeking asylum at the border. I had hoped that during the pandemic, our nation's leaders would come to see immigrants as more than just statistics, but rather as families and children struggling to make a life for themselves. But the discourse surrounding immigration reform continues to skew toward xenophobic stereotypes and chronic sidelining.

And though I did not think it was possible, the rhetoric has become even more brazenly derogatory. At a campaign rally for Donald Trump in Madison Square Garden in New York City, mere weeks before the election, a comedian likened the island of Puerto Rico to a "floating island of garbage." Compassionate leadership should include those who have worked hard to make the United States their home. Immigrants, naturalized or not (and in the case of Puerto Ricans, born citizens), are not a road-block to our country's prosperity; we only serve to amplify it.

Moving On from Grief

The intensity of 2020 proved to only be a taste of what was to come. Midway through his term as lieutenant governor in 2021, John announced that he would be running for the Senate. While he was busy campaigning, things were starting to feel more normal at home. We had reopened the Free Store, and I was bouncing between work, political events, and home. I attended the opening of a new dispensary, celebrated a birthday, and spent time with Bibi, who had returned from Brazil the previous summer, fresh off celebrating her ninety-fourth birthday. The kids were still learning remotely. When they weren't in school, sometimes they would tag along with me to the Free Store or to other initiatives we were running around town; on other days, they would hang out with Bibi and my mom. Though we were still social distancing and masking, my life felt full again, steeped in community.

Then, in May, Bibi had a stroke and had to be taken to the hospital. I spent every day with her, and in the halls of the hospital, I kept bumping into acquaintances. In the end, I ran into six people who were there for different reasons but also struggling. On May 3, Bibi died, two months before her ninety-fifth birthday. Her death devastated me. Bibi had been a constant presence in my and the kids' lives, and adjusting to living without her was and continues to be hard. I could not envision a new normal that did not include her peeling my grapes, stroking my hair, or making me laugh. She would often cook for the whole family, and the kids have memories of her making them cakes and other desserts. She made them the meringues she would make for me and my brother when we were younger. Meringues are laborious and hard to make, and when something went wrong, she would start from scratch and make a whole new batch to make sure I would have them on my birthday or other special occasions.

Two of the most important people in my life were gone within a year of each other. She had lost two children to the pandemic, including Tio Telmo, and it had changed her. While I took solace in the thought that she was reunited with them, I also felt a deep sense of *saudade*, which in Portuguese refers to a sense of melancholy and nostalgia. Her death felt like the loss of one of my lifelines for love, and every day I had to keep reminding myself that she was gone.

I am still working through this grief and have realized there is no quick or straightforward way to overcome it. But it has helped me—both in coping with these losses and other difficult experiences—to focus on small, pedestrian moments that spark joy. Like when my son August looked at me one day and told me he loved everything about me, including my smile and my wrinkles. Or when I noticed that whereas one of my dogs, Levi, used to jump right onto the couch, he started to lie at the bottom to let our other dog, Artie, use him as a support to get up first.

Artie only has three legs and was fresh from being rescued (and having a leg amputated) and was still learning how to get around. She was rescued from a dogfighting ring and lost her leg while being used as the bait dog.

Or when I ran into a flustered older woman in a rest stop bathroom who was getting ready to go on a date. I was washing my hands next to her and noticed that she had a spread of makeup on the shared counter. She looked stressed, as if she was trying to figure out where to start. Suddenly, she turned to me and asked, "Can you help me?" She revealed that she was going on her first date since her husband had died a decade ago. The cosmetics on the counter were all new, but she was overwhelmed and did not know how to apply them. I helped her make herself up, and when we parted, she was notably more relaxed than she had been when we started. I still think about her and hope she had a wonderful date.

When we are going through hard things, or when our loved ones are, it's important to allow ourselves moments of joy. Sometimes, when someone passes away, there is the expectation that we will be somber all the time—that we must wear our grief on our faces and bodies. Some may even judge us for laughing or smiling or wearing any color other than black, as if doing so somehow negates how we felt about the person we lost. But I reject that expectation. I believe these are the moments in which we need to lean further into joy so that we do not lose ourselves.

I'm inspired on this subject by Ross Gay, a writer and poet who has built his career on examining, studying, and writing about joy and delight. When he turned forty-two, he decided to write a mini-essay every day on something that delighted him. The result was *The Book of Delights,* in which he chronicled a year's worth of small joys: loitering, his friend's use of air quotes, his garden, the name tag on his friend's bag. "It didn't take me long to learn that the discipline or practice of writing these essays occasioned a kind of delight radar. Or maybe it was more like the development of a delight muscle," he writes. "Something that implies that the more you study delight, the more delight there is to study."

He found himself, in other words, oriented toward delight, more readily observing it in his daily life, even in unexpected places. In a conversation with Krista Tippett for the *On Being* podcast, he said that his preoccupation with delight is closely tied to an awareness of death. Despite a misconception that joy is easy, "joy has nothing to do with ease. And joy has everything to do with the fact that we're all going to die," he said. "When I'm thinking about joy, I'm thinking about that at the same time as something wonderful is happening, some connection is being made in my life, we are also in the process of dying." He adds, talking about the delightful things he encounters, "when they're there, they also imply their absence." As I was navigating Tio Telmo and Bibi's deaths, and later, when I would encounter other challenges, moving through the feelings that came up was made easier by making space for joy as well as sadness. I became more appreciative of what and who remained around me, and of life itself.

An opinion piece in *The New York Times* advocating for a delight practice (inspired by Gay) argued that this habit is particularly important in the face of all the darkness in the world, and that it can be good for us. "Noticing and sharing delight is also a form of what psychologists call savoring, the practice of deliberately appreciating positive life experiences," writes Catherine Price, who authored a book called *The Power of Fun.* "Savoring has been shown to boost people's moods as well as counterbalance our brains' natural tendency to focus on the things that stoke anxiety and fear."

When we deny ourselves joy, we are making more room for darkness. We are also denying ourselves an opportunity for connection. Price mentions in the article that she has created group chats dedicated to pointing out delights, and says it makes her feel closer to friends who share the small things that bring them joy on a daily basis. "And what might it do to the country's political climate if we paid less attention to the things that divide us and more to the things that spark delight?" Price ponders, concluding, "It's possible to disagree with people, to acknowledge life's challenges, to debate, to sit with sadness, grief and fear while marveling at and seeking out simple joys."

I, too, wonder how our world could shift if we focused on the beauty we encounter rather than on the arbitrary walls we've put up to separate us. How might it change how we feel about ourselves? How might it change the way we treat each other? The way we treat women or people who have less than us? How we treat those who can do nothing for us? Living through and being fortunate enough to survive the pandemic made me more committed than ever to this practice, which would prove useful for tackling what was to come.

CHAPTER 7

REDEFINING STRENGTH

J ohn was getting a lot of great statewide and even national attention for his work as lieutenant governor of Pennsylvania. With a Pennsylvania Senate seat opening up in 2022, John made the decision to run. It was going to be a tough race, but we had a sense he could thrive and make a difference on this, an even larger stage. As a family we took a collective breath, and then took a leap.

In May 2022, mere days ahead of the Democratic primary for the open Senate seat, John and I were stopped at a gas station in Lancaster, Pennsylvania. All of a sudden, I saw the side of his mouth droop as we were getting into the car. It was a slight movement, imperceptible to anyone not paying attention. But I could tell something was wrong. I insisted we go to the hospital.

John pushed back. We were between events, he said, insisting that time was of the essence in this campaign, and every appearance was crucial. And because no one had seen what I had, the state troopers, who accompanied us everywhere we went, were confused. "Ma'am, he seems fine," one of them told me. There were no other indications that something was awry. When you think of a stroke, you think of someone not being able to speak or losing control of parts of their body. But John's speech was perfect. He didn't seem sick, and his mouth quickly resumed its natural position. He also did not seem to have felt any change himself. No one would be blamed for letting it go. But I just knew that the movement his mouth made is one he could not have made on his own. It felt unnatural, and I could not shake the feeling that something was wrong.

We pushed through, against John's wishes. The troopers redirected the GPS, and we headed to the nearest emergency room instead of his scheduled event. The whole way to the hospital, John kept saying, "She's crazy. I don't know what she's talking about." It was hard even getting him in the door. "I'm fine," he kept telling the troopers. But sure enough, at the hospital, a doctor told us John had suffered a stroke. They told us that he would need surgery to remove a clot that had formed during an episode of atrial fibrillation, which meant that the bottom and top chambers of his heart were out of sync. A few days later, they also installed a pacemaker and defibrillator to treat a diagnosis of cardiomyopathy.

I was there in the hospital with John for three days straight. Didn't shower; didn't eat. I was consumed by worry and some frustration; there had been indications that something was wrong with John's heart since 2017, but he had never done any follow-up care. It was a huge shock to all of us, and the kids found out about their dad's condition only a few minutes before we told the press. I kept thinking how close a call it had been. Had I not noticed he was slightly "off," he might have been at risk for a more severe stroke later on, or even death.

I spent those days by his side. On Election Day, when it was announced that John had won the primary and would compete in the general election later that fall, he had just gotten out of surgery. The troopers drove me three hours home, where I quickly got ready and headed to the election party. I gave the victory speech on his behalf and accepted the congratulatory call from President Biden.

Over the coming weeks and months, I would continue to support and sometimes serve as a surrogate for him at campaign events. I had already become used to these sorts of public appearances as SLOP, but the vulnerability of having to juggle John's political commitments with supporting my children and John as he recovered meant that I felt teary more often. It was not unusual for me to cry during media interviews, which reporters often noted in their stories.

"Politics is mean and hard, and Gisele—soft Gisele, who cries three times over the course of this interview—had no choice but to get good at it," wrote one reporter, who also noted, elsewhere in the article: "A thick skin isn't soft. And Gisele could use a thicker skin these days." She pointed out all that was getting to me in that moment: "the attacks from her husband's opponent, former TV doctor Mehmet Oz; the disdainful comments she hears from people who fixate on her past as an undocumented immigrant. Piled onto that are all the injustices of life in America in 2022. Oh, and also the puppies." (The writer was referring to a Jezebel report that found that Dr. Oz's medical experiments had caused the deaths of more than three hundred dogs.)

Perhaps there are some who think I should have kept my composure or not shown that I was overwhelmed, but it was less important to me to keep up appearances than it was to get through those days, when so much was in flux. What followed would be a lesson in both the perils and benefits of vulnerability on such a large scale.

Live for Today

It was not the first time that I had made this sort of lifesaving catch. The first time involved my daughter, Grace, and it started with a photograph—or a series of photographs, if I'm to be exact. Like any new mom, I spent a lot of time photographing my children's every move. They seemed not to have any bad angles in my eyes, every new gesture or expression worthy of being memorialized. One day, the kids at school, I opened my laptop and started uploading the latest batch. That's when I noticed something strange. In all the pictures in which the flash caused my children's eyes to turn red, my daughter had a singular yellow eye. Always the same eye. Always five red eyes and one yellow.

Alarms went off. By my quasi-scientific reasoning, if red eyes were the result of red blood vessels being illuminated by the camera's flash, did that not mean something could be wrong with the blood circulation in my daughter's eye? A quick online search did nothing to assuage my worries. Eventually, I came across a website for an organization called Know the Glow, which raises awareness about the implications of the yellow glow I was seeing in my daughter's pictures. There were maybe five possible things that could be happening to my daughter, and none of them were positive: cataracts, retinal detachment, a tumor, cancer, or Coats disease.

Immediately I looked up a specialty eye doctor, learned this person was called an ophthalmologist, and called their office. A bright receptionist picked up the phone.

"I don't want to be an alarmist," I told her, "but I've noticed that my daughter's eye is yellow in every single picture I've taken of her recently. I want to know if I should be worried."

"Please hold," she said, after a brief pause. "I'll connect you to the doctor."

When he came to the phone, the doctor's voice sounded grave and serious. "Pull her out of school and bring her in immediately," he told me.

Perhaps this is strange, but though it is scary to think back on this, in the moment I felt a surprising sense of calm. I knew I had a job to do. At the doctor's office, John was so worried that he couldn't even get out of the car. I don't blame him for feeling scared and overwhelmed. But I went into a sort of autopilot as my daughter underwent testing. On the way to the doctor's office, I told her where we were going and why. I showed her the photos and explained that there might be something wrong, and we were going to get it checked.

"It's probably nothing, but if there is something wrong, we'll figure it out together," I said.

This wasn't just lip service. When I face high-stress situations like that one, I try to prepare for neither the worst nor the best, because anything could happen. I believe you need to go into situations completely open, and that means accepting that the outcome might not make you feel good. I believed then and do now that whatever the outcome, we could get through it as a family. This steadfast belief makes it so that there is little that really shocks or surprises. Anything can happen, and there's peace in acknowledging it.

We soon learned that my daughter had Coats disease, a rare disorder that causes blood vessels to expand and leak fluid into the retina. If left untreated, she could have lost vision in the eye altogether. She was only in kindergarten, still learning letters, so it was unlikely a regular eye exam would have detected any issue. The doctor prescribed corrective lenses that needed to be monitored and swapped out every couple of weeks. She also had to do eye exercises.

It is inevitable that life will come with these sorts of challenges. I'm very grateful for the outcome that we had, and afterward, I wanted to try to help others identify this preventable issue early. A couple years later, once she was recovered, my daughter and I appeared on local and national news to talk about her experience and help others recognize the glow. My thought was that, if even just one more person could learn to recognize the signs, it would prevent another family from suffering. If I learn information that helps someone else, the only response that makes sense to me is to share it. And also to send the message that, even when things seem hard, we can overcome whatever life throws at us.

That I noticed the change in my daughter's eye was one part luck and one part a reflection of my approach to relationships. I'm someone who is obsessed with the present. It's nice to plan for the future and reminisce about the past, sure, but I find that living in either space for too long takes away from the most important time in our lives. Whenever I am with someone, I might as well have blinders on—I think and pour into only them, giving them all my attention. This allows me to notice things that others might not. I register the slightest changes, because I never stop paying attention. It is my superpower: a hyperawareness of the physical, emotional, and energetic shifts of those around me in that moment.

When you know people well, overwhelm them with love and attention, it's easier to spot when something is wrong. This is a trait that Dr. Elaine N. Aron points to in *The Highly Sensitive Person: How to Thrive When the World Overwhelms You*, in which she writes about the traits that define people with a preternatural inclination toward sensitivity, both emotional and in terms of social stimuli. Highly sensitive people, she writes, "pick up on the subtleties that others miss." I'm not sure if I would be considered a highly sensitive person *technically*, but my attunement to the world around me makes it so that I pick up on cues others might not. Noticing the small change in John's expression saved his life. Realizing that something was off with my daughter's eye prevented her from going blind or developing further complications.

There is a lot of value in staying aware and in tune with the present. I do not catastrophize or burden myself by imagining worst-case scenarios that may or may not come true. I face situations as they come and ensure that those around me have what they need and are well taken care of. In addition to the service I provide for others, I practice staying present by nourishing my own creativity—projects that force me to focus and lock in for long periods of time. Recently, I created a planter out of an old file cabinet that was going to be thrown away. I often create mosaics, big and small, to donate or gift to people I meet. Those moments nourish us and allow us to relish what the present has to offer us. We learn to stay in place so we don't miss things that might otherwise pass us by. We are meant to slow down; to take things in; to thoughtfully consider our surroundings and circumstances. That is our gift to the world and to the people with whom we interact. In other words, sensitivity has its own role to play.

The Burden of Womanhood

In response to my increased presence on the campaign trail, right-wing media lodged sexist attacks at me, blaming me for "letting" John continue his campaign or painting me as an opportunist trying to take his spot. The former was incredibly sexist, a continuation of a long tradition of blaming women for the actions of men, and the latter was a ludicrous conspiracy theory. Even a decade-long tradition of cutting John's head off on photos posted to my social media—he's so tall that I often have to choose between featuring him or my shoes, and the shoes often win out!—was twisted as a power grab, with many painting me as a self-absorbed wife obsessed with centering myself. If before I had been a shortcut to get to John, I was now a punching bag and scapegoat for those who disagreed with his decisions.

I talk about this a lot with Connie Schultz, the wife of former Ohio senator Sherrod Brown, who experienced some of the same and touches on it in her book, *And His Lovely Wife: A Memoir from the Woman Beside the Man*. We've seen how women politicians are lampooned in the media, and the wives of politicians are not exempt from this sort of treatment. Anyone unhappy with John felt entitled to shift blame onto me, as if I was somehow responsible for steering his career. I'm sure my age, race, and online presence make me particularly vulnerable to these attacks. Connie was always a willing and generous listener, someone who could speak from experience about what I was encountering. Whenever I called her because someone had attacked me for one of John's stances or because another off-the-wall story had been published, she told me about instances in which she had experienced the same.

"This is not your role," she often reminded me. "You don't speak for him, and you shouldn't feel like you have to."

At home, we were dealing with how to adapt to our new reality. John was recovering, but the effects of his stroke and the aftermath were lingering. For one thing, he had developed an auditory processing disorder that affected his ability to fully hear what others were saying to him. We had to make accommodations for how we engaged with him, going to movies with closed captioning devices available and using a voice-to-text app for him to communicate with the kids when there was too much background noise. It felt natural to us that we would make these changes, and no one in the family felt burdened or upset. I was proud to see the love and patience with which the children quickly adapted.

But so much of our experience was complicated by having our lives open for the public to criticize and dissect. When he did start to make appearances again, John relied on assistive closed captioning technology for interviews. His opponent for the Pennsylvania Senate seat, Mehmet Oz, took this opportunity to paint him as weak and unfit for office, and this narrative was quickly picked up by right-wing media. I even received personal messages mocking his speech. The whole thing struck me as incredibly ableist and contrary to how my family was experiencing his recovery: as a success story. The difference between the uncharitable way the public viewed our personal crisis and the supportive way we were adapting to it as a family was striking. Though I tried to shield them as best I could, my kids saw a lot of the coverage criticizing and attacking John. They were as appalled as I was. They recognized the poor behavior of adults and were very upset by it.

What was most surprising was how even liberal media organizations covered his condition, seemingly latching on to Oz's rhetoric that the campaign was being dishonest about John's condition or fitness to serve. Rebecca Traister, a political reporter for *New York* magazine, put it perfectly in a profile of John around this time, pointing out that "legitimate newspapers are pushing for further documentation with some of the energy once applied to Hillary's emails, while the right-wing carnival barkers treat complete medical records as they did Obama's birth certificate." As Traister pointed out in her article (and I felt at the time), these continued requests were baffling, because as I saw it, we were being as transparent as we could possibly be, releasing information as soon as we had a conclusive diagnosis. In addition to official communications from his campaign, on May 15, two days after the stroke, I posted several videos and photos on Instagram explaining what had happened and sharing what we knew. Nothing was hidden from the public. These attacks and the constant badgering were merely an effort to undermine his campaign.

Amid all of this, I was showing up where I needed to be and trying to support John's campaign as best I could. I had to both process my feelings and respond to questions, requests, and criticisms from the public in real time. While I was horrified by how the media was painting both John and me, when we were both doing the best we could, it was also not my most pressing concern. That I might develop a negative reputation for how I was responding was not as important as getting through each day. People really care and are attached to their reputations, but that is not how I was raised by my Bibi and my mother. I was taught to be who I was unapologetically and not care about the rest. I do not covet having a good reputation. And I was not interested in putting on a mask that might make me more palatable.

Of more import to me was managing my own feelings and that of my children. And in this difficult moment, I used my feelings to fuel me. This did not feel like a moment to shut off my emotions but rather a moment to lean in and feel the enormity of, well, *everything*. To me, embracing emotion is necessary to staying present and awake to current circumstances. A childhood filled with change and adaptation forced this lesson on me: that I needed to release and process to remain optimistic about the future.

Public vulnerability is often viewed as embarrassing or "cringe"—particularly in politics, in which maintaining composure is baked into the job description. Because John is a public figure, we had no choice about whether what our family was going through could remain behind closed doors. But I did have a choice in the value that I placed on others' opinions, and it was very little.

Public Vulnerability

I had begun to feel concerned about John's mental health in the months leading up to the November Senate election. His mood started to shift after a publicized debate with Oz in October 2022. He had been behaving less and less like himself. He always had a melancholic side to him, but this time around, his sadness seemed acute, compounded by the aftereffects of his health crisis, which was causing him deep distress. John refused to leave our bedroom and seemed zoned out when I or the kids tried to speak with him. He kept telling me he was fine, but it was clear that he wasn't.

I thought that once the grueling race was over, win or lose, and he was free from the stress of campaigning, that he would return to his old self. John managed a historic victory, winning all sixty-seven counties in Pennsylvania. But after he won, he seemed sadder than ever.

The final straw was when he learned that a reporter who he had connected with over their shared experience of surviving a stroke—a person who had given him hope for a full recovery— had died by suicide. We learned later that depression is common in the year after a stroke, and in John's case, his experience was exacerbated by having to balance his recovery with the intensity of campaigning. In early February, I finally told him, "John, if something happens and you die tomorrow, the kids are going to remember you as a really sad person. Is that what you want?" He knew I was serious because I called him John rather than João, my Portuguese nickname for him. I only called him John when I was upset or wanted to make a point. Thankfully, my concern sunk in. And the next day, less than two months into his term, he checked himself into Walter Reed Medical Center to treat his clinical depression. His official check-in date was our eldest son Karl's birthday.

The media attention was unbearable. The day he checked into the hospital, I peeked out my window to see that there were news crews circling my home. I packed up the kids and drove with no destination in mind—just wanting to go somewhere away from all the attention, somewhere we could be together in peace. We ended up in Toronto, which gave me four hours of driving to answer all their questions on the way up. We zip-lined over Niagara Falls and August got stuck midway. We cried and we laughed. Coping with mental health challenges in a public setting opened John (and me) up to ridicule and intense criticism. Some Republican lawmakers and commentators went as far as to say that he was unfit to serve in the Senate, as if treating a medical issue made him less capable of doing his job. At the same time, I was criticized for my choice to "leave the country" for two days with the kids, and the conspiracy theory about me plotting to steal John's Senate seat persisted. Shortly after John admitted himself into Walter Reed, a Twitter poll put up by a conservative commentator had followers vote between Jada Pinkett Smith, Meghan Markle, Jill Biden, and me for "worst wife in America." It's worth noting here that, quite predictably, three out of the four candidates were women of color.

It was the first time a politician had been so quickly and publicly vulnerable about depression or mental health challenges, so while some media attention was not surprising, I did not expect it to skew toward such cruelty. My main concern was giving my children some distance—making sure that they had the space to process what was happening and reassuring them that John would be OK. Looking out at the falls, I explained that Dad was suffering and was working hard to get better. I told them how proud of him I was. I told them that Dad loved them and wanted to be fully present for them; that he needed to take care of himself to be an even better parent. I told them we would see him as soon as possible.

Caring for one's mental health is often viewed as a form of weakness, a sign that one cannot handle the pressures of the world. There is still a taboo around speaking openly about mental health challenges or seeking support. According to the Centers for Disease Control and Prevention, less than a quarter of Americans received mental health treatment in 2020, and culturally, we still have not overcome our understanding of therapy as something embarrassing or that betrays our weakness. This is especially true among men, who lag behind women in seeking out care.

But there is no denying its benefits. When John came back home, six weeks later, he was back to his old self and better than ever—fully engaged with the kids, back to his early mornings, and ready to do his work enthusiastically. The moment I realized John—the João I know and love—was back with us was when he started to express gratitude again, for his second chance, the time to heal, and his family that had been waiting for him back at home. His outlook had become more positive, a complete 180 compared to before his treatment.

Bottom line: Mental health treatment is necessary to build resilience and prepare us to face life's challenges. It's something we prioritize as a family, and it's something I take care of myself as a wife, mother, daughter, and individual. I would not be able to deal with the criticism and hate I receive if I didn't take the time to work out my own issues.

Because of John's willingness to be open about his medical struggles, I've received countless messages asking me for advice on how to support a spouse going through a similar medical crisis. I heard stories from people suffering from intrusive suicidal thoughts, depression, and schizophrenia. I heard from people who had lost loved ones to suicide.

Being vulnerable in public spaces is its own form of leadership. In *The Highly Sensitive Person,* Dr. Aron reframes the value of vulnerability and sensitivity in our society, arguing that the role highly sensitive people play is complementary to aggression and necessary in public spaces. People who possess this trait, she writes, "were born to be among the advisors and thinkers, the spiritual and moral leaders of your society." When we allow ourselves to be vulnerable, we serve as an example of a different way of moving through the world that does not center silencing our feelings or perpetuating harm. We pay it forward, teaching compassion and giving room for other people to do the same. Living my life out loud is a way of extending empathy, holding out a hand to others who might be too afraid to speak up otherwise. I do so to destigmatize difficult topics and allow others to do the same. That's why I have been open about my ADHD diagnosis at thirty-eight (women are notoriously underdiagnosed or treated late) and other aspects of my personal life. This is all a part of my story, of who I am, and not sharing it would be to deny myself my full humanity.

Oh, and that Twitter poll about the worst wife? I lost to Jada Pinkett Smith, earning just 14 percent of the vote. Ah well, you can't win them all. In an Instagram story, I responded in jest, saying: "LOL, Only I get to call myself that!" And a year after the poll results were posted, in early 2024, I celebrated its anniversary on my Twitter account, noting that it "feels like yesterday that I was up for this prestigious award."

Inverting Social Norms

Right around the time that all this was happening, I decided to enter the fire academy. Often, women are forced to set aside their dreams in support of their husbands' careers or to prioritize their families, and while I was grateful to be able to support John during the campaign, I wanted to do something that was just for me. Firefighting was a dream I'd once held and had long since forgotten. I was approaching forty when Mom decided to downsize and started going through stuff she'd accumulated since my brother and I were kids: old journals filled with poetry, photographs, and other memorabilia. She came across an old yearbook of mine, and underneath my name, I saw that little me had once wanted to be a firefighter. Somewhere along the way, subconsciously, I must have convinced myself that it was not attainable for me—that I wasn't strong or tough enough to run into a burning building. But being confronted with my childhood aspiration helped me tap into that little girl's fearlessness, and soon I cast away my worries and enrolled in the fire academy and signed to run with the Rivers Edge 113 Volunteer Fire Department.

I was the oldest person in my cohort and one of few women. I became the academy mom, making sure everyone stayed hydrated and had plenty of snacks. The training was physically and emotionally taxing. For months, I spent several days a week going through four levels of essential training and learning how to take proper care of myself and my fellow first responders. We were trained in endurance and CPR, and we spent hours actively putting out fires. I had to cut holes in roofs and rescue a dummy that was at least twice my weight by carrying it out the window of a building. Finally, in May 2023, I was cleared as an interior firefighter.

Participating in and completing the academy was a thrill and made me feel more capable. When my service was reported by the media, many of the comments were mocking, calling the move a public relations stunt or saying that I might break a nail. (For the record, I garden and create glass art; my nails are regularly unkempt.) Many doubted I would put in any hours at the station and assumed I was only in it for the photo op.

But in 2023, I responded to more than 100 calls. And in 2024, 150 and counting. I report to duty whenever I am in town and have been at the scene for a number of challenging calls.

I view firefighting as an extension of service work—a chance to show up for my community members on their worst days. Often, because I meet so many people at the Free Store, I know the people whose calls we are responding to. I feel an immense privilege to be able to serve my community this way. Our work extends beyond active fires. We get called in after shootings, to car crashes, and for wellness checks. If we are there, it means something terrible has or is about to happen. This sort of work can be distressing, to say the least. Given the brutal nature of the scenes that firefighters are often called into, many are left with lingering trauma that has long-term impact, with suicide being among the top causes of death among firefighters. But my sensitivity has not held me back from doing this work. Instead, it has helped me empathize with victims and serve as an example for young girls who have never seen a woman working as a firefighter.

The experience has reaffirmed that sensitivity is not the limiting trait many perceive it to be. Before joining the department, I had heard stories about displays of mental and physical toughness being elevated to points of pride. I expected shows of male bravado, chauvinism, or worse. But I lucked out with my station, which is quite the opposite and where we are mutually supportive. I get to work with the most incredible people. There is no gatekeeping at my station. Every officer is generous with their time and knowledge. After difficult calls, my fellow firefighters check in on me and one another. One of them—Uncle Nick—is a senior firefighter who's been on the job for forty years and looks out for me as if I were his daughter. Recently, he said to me, "You know, Gisele, you've exceeded all expectations. I'm really proud of you." It meant a great deal to hear that from someone I deeply admire.

There are still times when my colleagues worry about me on particularly difficult calls, because they know how sensitive I am. But by continuing to show up, I prove to myself and others that tenderness is not a hindrance to this work. You can be sensitive and still do hard things—even if you have to go home and cry after. Though there is a level of compartmentalization that needs to happen to do this work, I allow myself space to grieve losses and process traumatic incidents. I know the consequences of letting these feelings go unchecked.

One day, we responded to a fire at a single-family house. Nobody was home, so by the time anybody noticed the blaze, it had seeped into the walls and insulation. When we arrived, the fire was beginning to spread to the house next door. Soon after, the young woman who lived next door arrived, understandably distraught—and I immediately realized that I knew her mom. Or rather, I had *known* her mom, a wonderful lady who had recently passed away from cancer. The mom had been diagnosed with cancer young—in her forties—and she had been in remission for a brief period before the disease came back, stronger, and it progressed very quickly. She was survived by two daughters, one twenty-one (whose home was beginning to burn) and the other six years old. It was so sad; another tragedy visiting this young girl and her family.

I also knew that, before passing, this woman had recorded her voice saying "I love you" in a Build-a-Bear unicorn. Which was currently in this burning house. I knew this was probably the second worst day of her life—after losing her mom—and I could not bear to see her lose that gift from her mom, too. I alerted the team that the unicorn needed to be rescued, and everyone came together to ensure that it found its way safely back to her. I hope that the unicorn (and her mom's voice) offered some comfort.

CHAPTER 8

WHY TENDERNESS = LEADERSHIP

Since John was elected senator, I have found myself in rooms and with people I never could have imagined I would meet. It's easy to get swept up in that—to think being in those rooms makes you smarter or more impressive than others. Or the opposite: that you don't deserve to be there. Politics is a space in which appearances and decorum matter, and for those who do not look like the majority, the social norms and expectations within the political sphere may not match their own. But after all the challenges of the pandemic—both my personal and our collective losses—as well as seeing John through his health crises, I felt prepared to take it all in stride.

In Brazil, I grew up hearing about *jeitinho brasileiro*, or the Brazilian way. It's a social philosophy and approach to life defined by flexibility and ingenuity. The idea is that with a little wiggle, charm, and finesse, you can work your way out of or into any situation—even if it requires bending the rules a bit.

I tried to approach my new life in the public eye that way, molding it to my values and temperament rather than the other way around. To me, *jeitinho brasileiro* is also about not taking yourself too seriously. I take people seriously. I take the work I do seriously, but I do not place too much stock in how I come off or how I'm perceived. Embodying *jeitinho brasileiro* has made it easier for me to navigate these spaces, because rather than feel out of place, I eschew cultural expectations, embrace rejection, and try to have fun. Part of that is delusion—I'm aware that there are sometimes people around me who might not respect me, or take me seriously—but so long as it helps me move in a positive and confident way, I am fine with it.

At this point, I've met countless senators, current and former presidents, celebrities, and other so-called VIPs. I always talk to them respectfully but casually. On a plane with President Barack Obama, we ate pancakes and talked about music. I often walk down the halls of the Capitol building playfully exclaiming, "There's my favorite senator!" to anyone I meet (minus the ones that are not great). When someone complimented me on the dress I wore to the first day of spousal orientation in D.C., I proudly told them, "Thanks! It's thrifted. Twelve dollars!" Despite getting criticism for it, I kept choosing my shoes over John's head in photographs. So much of politics can be boring and stiff; I do not want to lean into that. Part of that is letting go of self-consciousness and focusing on personal connections and interests rather than status.

The first year that I was invited to the White House Correspondents' Association Dinner, I saw on the guest list that the cast of *Vanderpump Rules* would be there. I'm a huge fan of the show, which follows Lisa Vanderpump and the staff at her various restaurants. Reality shows more generally appeal to me because the cast members volunteer to live their lives, however chaotic and messy, publicly. It's a bold and brave choice. So, out of all the names on the list of attendees, I was most excited to meet the cast of the show, especially Ariana Madix. I said as much, without hesitation, when I was interviewed by a Serious News Show ahead of the event and asked who I was looking forward to meeting. When I arrived, I went straight to their table and told them what I had told the news anchor. They seemed pleasantly surprised. I always tell John, "I'll come to D.C. if it's something fun!" Of course, I show up if it's important, but I do not want to get caught up in that world. It does not interest me.

When John was still campaigning, we had an event in Philadelphia with President Biden, who invited us onto Air Force One. Before getting to ride on the plane, I had heard this rumor that it was stocked with M&M's that had the presidential seal. As soon as we entered, instead of asking about the important events or places where the plane had taken him or the latest congressional hearing, I said, "Pres, I heard there are presidential M&M's." He laughed and told me that there were before offering me some.

"How many can I have?" I asked him.

"As many as you want," he answered, his eyes twinkling with laughter.

I'm sure he didn't imagine that I would ask to take the whole basket. President Biden was caught off guard but laughed and encouraged me to take them all.

This may not have been proper decorum, but it's not every day that you get to ride on Air Force One, and it was much more meaningful to me to be able to share the experience with my colleagues at the Free Store. I did not play it cool and pretend like I wasn't excited about riding the presidential plane, or about calling my mom from the air, or about the little boxes of M&M's that bore the president's signature. It's important to really be present and take in experiences fully.

Centering the Vulnerable

The woman came into the Free Store holding a large black garbage bag. It seemed packed to the brim, as if she'd emptied out her closet and brought it to our store. It was clear almost immediately that she had lost someone. Her demeanor was solemn, and she clutched the bag as if reluctant to let it go.

We are often the last stop for people who have just lost a loved one. They come in after going through the painful process of sorting through belongings of the deceased, deciding what to toss and what to rehome. It is one of the many ways we get to be a part of these very tender and vulnerable spaces in their lives. One of our volunteers, Mr. Walt, who had lost his son to a stroke, had been bringing in items little by little. Every time he came in, he would bring a few more things with which he was ready to part.

We learned that this woman's son had died by suicide. He was only in his midtwenties when he passed, and she was the one who had found him. For years, his things had sat untouched; she couldn't bear to say goodbye to the last connection she had to him. That day, she had finally mustered the courage and strength.

"May I help put things on hangers?" she asked.

We brought out hangers, and with each item she pulled out, she would share a memory. "He wore this to his graduation."

"He wore this the last time we went out to dinner."

Everybody was crying. It was beautiful and sad. As she was working, a man walked into the store who lived in the halfway house in town. It offers a transitional home and support for men who are just out of prison and trying to get their lives back on track. Many are from other states or don't have family support, and a lot of them frequent our store.

When the man walked in, the grieving mother asked his size. When he told her, she said, "I think you're my son's size." She started offering him clothes. Picking up a bowling-style striped shirt, she said, "I think you would look so handsome in this." She gave him a suit that he said he would wear to a job interview. The man walked out with a wardrobe of clothes; the woman left lighter than when she had arrived. Everyone there that day cried.

People around me balked when I told them I would be opening a store where everything would be free. Where our inventory would be built through donations, and our workers—who are all volunteers—would not have to worry about theft or ringing anyone up or getting contact information. Where we would not worry about profits or bottom lines but would merely serve as a vehicle for seeing that items go where they are needed.

I was told people would take advantage of the system. It's the sort of thing that does not make sense in a capitalist society, they informed me. But I was inspired by the free stores of the 1960s, which originated in San Francisco at a time when mutual aid, peace, and cooperation were ever-popular philosophies. A lot of places that give away free goods require that people fill out a form, but I decided early on that I wouldn't do that. I had no interest in collecting patrons' contact information or having them prove that they "actually" needed the help we were offering. What I wanted was to offer a dignified experience—for no one to feel less than after walking through our doors. If you need something and we have it, you're welcome to take it.

Today, the Free Store is like my church. I always say that if you're losing hope or faith in humanity, you should come hang out at the Free Store. Interactions like the one I describe above happen frequently there. We've had shoppers become donors or volunteers—people who came in years ago with nothing and come back to pay it forward, dropping off diapers, baby clothes, or other items. I know kids whose moms brought them in as babies, who are now in high school. We see retired folks on a fixed income who are raising their grandchildren. Refugees from countries in the Middle East who helped the United States during the Iraq War. Everyone is equal and welcome, and we don't turn anyone away. I think we have such low expectations of one another that we expect the worst. At the Free Store, we've been able to show that you can believe in people. We've created a space for those who are willing to help others. It's the place where all my values are brought to bear and the one place where I can shape and decide how people treat one another.

Everyone Deserves a Second Chance

We have only a few rules at the Free Store: Be kind. Make a new friend. Take only what you need. Pay it forward. I think these are significant, easy lessons for life. Before the Free Store, I had not led a team of people since college, back when I was in the financial auditing sector. Back then, being a manager did not feel particularly challenging. Being good to people came naturally to me, and I liked the way I could lean into that as a manager. I got to cheer people on, inspire and be inspired by them, and work to get the best out of them. Though in the financial-auditing days, I had no say over the company culture (which was, at times, *problematic*), I did have agency over how I ran my team.

The Free Store was a different story. This was the very first place where I was in complete control of the culture and environment I wanted to foster. I knew early on that I did not want to promote the same sort of culture that exists in many other workplaces, in which there is little flexibility and an emphasis on hierarchy. And I had never responded to much of the advice given in management courses. A lot of it seemed to boil down to: *You are in charge. You have to demand respect in how people address and speak to you.* This sort of guidance made me quite uncomfortable.

My foundation for management has nothing to do with enforcing authority. Beyond the basic respect that everyone is owed, I have no interest in dictating how my teammates engage with me or limiting what I "allow." Instead, my focus is on instilling trust in people, acknowledging them, and inspiring them. I ask for their suggestions and implement their ideas. I listen to them and seriously consider their suggestions, ideas, and visions. At first, when people would come into the Free Store and ask who was in charge, people would say, "Gisele." But now they say, "We all are."

The same generosity and care that I offer to patrons, I offer to my volunteers. I prioritize making our volunteers feel loved and listened to, seen and appreciated. Many have been with us since we opened in 2012 and are from all walks of life: retirees, people recovering from drug dependency, disabled folks, and more. No matter what your story is, we open our doors to those who want a second chance.

It's not always easy. Because the Free Store is open to anyone and everyone, all sorts of personalities come through there. Most days, its patrons confirm my view of the world: that everyone possesses inherent goodness and will show their best if given the chance. But I also often witness how unresolved trauma can explode into misunderstandings and altercations, just as it sometimes did in my neighborhood in New Jersey growing up. Visitors to the Free Store often live on edge and in survival mode, as I once did, which leaves little room for emotional probing. They do not always have the bandwidth to expand their purview past today.

At least once or twice per week, small conflicts elicit oversized reactions or blow up into heated arguments, whether because someone cut another person in line, stepped on their shoes, or spoke with a supposed attitude. I often interrupt these interactions by pulling those involved outside and trying to help them connect. I introduce them to each other and have them play the "Just Like Me" game, asking them to raise their hands if a statement applies to them.

"Raise your hand if you like tacos!"

"Raise your hand if you're a parent!"

"Raise your hand if you're having a rough day."

If they can relate, I instruct the patrons to say, "Oh, just like me!" as they raise their hands. At first, people get annoyed. I'm sure I seem like a kindergarten teacher. But most of the time, turning the clash into a silly interaction squashes the conflict and elicits an apology. People are embarrassed by their reaction once they calm down and pause. I've seen friendships develop from these sorts of conflicts.

But there are times when the volunteers get frustrated or exhausted. All my volunteers have lived or are living through their own challenges, many of which echo those of the community who use the store. They're all lovely, kind, and generous people, but the work we do requires patience and empathy, and it's often hard to offer that when you're facing your own challenges. They often jokingly call me the Zen master. If a visitor is in a bad mood, I tell them, "Regardless of how they behave, they're just people who want to be loved, just like you and me."

One of our volunteers, Mel, who used to be really feisty, says that things don't really bother her anymore. Anytime someone acts up, she'll say, "I know, Gisele, *they're someone who wants to be loved.*" It's my way of pushing people to think differently and approach things with their whole heart.

Because of the nature of our work, there is a lot more leniency and flexibility in what is allowed and expected from volunteers. And because many have been volunteering with us for years, we are really a family, and I worry about and miss them on days we are not together. That's why it hurt when we lost one of our volunteers to addiction. Stefanie was wonderful and fun, and great with customers; she would always get down and put shoes on kids or help them find sizes. But some days, I knew her bottle of water was not filled with water. We knew she struggled with alcohol dependency, but it mostly did not affect her job. Of course, we wished she wasn't drinking, but I think for us it was more important to have her there with us.

When she didn't show up, we were always worried. She said her work at the Free Store was the only thing that got her out of bed some mornings. We lost her after a hard-fought battle with addiction. We miss her and think of her often. I'm glad that, even if for a brief time, we were able to offer her a sense of stability and belonging. I believe flexibility is important. Even on days when she showed up intoxicated, we were happy to see her.

She needed a place to accept her as she was while she struggled to change. We believe in second chances and have a reputation for being a safe, loving, and welcoming space.

Ours is not a corporate environment, but we do have a standard for how we receive those who visit us. For me, it's important that every experience patrons have at the Free Store is positive. We're there to offer people love and support, and serve as a Band-Aid during a hard time.

Often, the guys from the halfway house will come and ask to volunteer with us. They will say, "We hear so-and-so had a really nice time with you all." They talk to one another about their experience with us, and then others come. Formerly incarcerated people have very little support when they get out. Often, people are quick to pass judgment without knowing their full stories or the circumstances behind their arrests. At the Free Store, we try to rally around them and offer our support, but what hope is there for people who don't have a family or a village?

Society is angry when formerly incarcerated people reoffend, but we are not doing enough to remove the barriers they often face to employment or housing. We ostracize them without knowing their full stories. I think many people believe that if someone has committed a crime, that's what they're destined for—they're not going to get or be better. But these are lies we've been told that pit us against one another and come between us. If we want people who were imprisoned to succeed in reincorporating themselves into society, we all must commit to being part of that process. We should all be rooting for them. They're going to be our neighbors. Don't we want them to be the best versions of themselves? Shouldn't we give them the opportunity to be a good neighbor? We have had guys come help with landscaping or stocking. Though we are not able to add to our roster of regular volunteers, anyone who wants to help on a one-off basis, we find a way to involve. We all have gifts to share with the world that are all different and all needed.

When I was Second Lady, I did a tour of prisons in Pennsylvania. I was trying to change the system and allow imprisoned people to be in plainclothes when their children came to visit. It makes a big difference in the confidence of the person and how they perceive themselves, and, in many cases, they might get more visitors. Though we did not get there, I think it is a small change that could have a big impact. There was no consistency across prisons, and the quality of life was based on who the warden was. In some, inmates were taking yoga and going to college, while in others, there were limited options for self-improvement. It was a crapshoot, and what they learned while incarcerated (and their opportunities for success after they were released) varied wildly.

I believe that we work against the formerly incarcerated—and our society's best interest—by not giving every incarcerated person the best possible chance at success when they get out. As of this writing, fifteen states and thirty-seven cities and counties have passed Ban the Box legislation, which prohibits employers from asking applicants to disclose criminal history before having been evaluated on their merits. For the most part, this has been limited to the public sector, but twenty-two of these localities have extended the regulations to the private sector. This opens the door for more people who would otherwise be qualified for a position but are shut out by discriminatory hiring practices. It also fills a need for employers struggling to recruit new talent. Rooting for people is never a bad thing.

Become Friendly with Failure

Part of revolutionizing how we approach tenderness at work is embracing failure, or rather, reframing our perception of it. I'm impulsive and often jump into things without considering whether I will succeed. Some might be discouraged as soon as something goes wrong or things don't go as planned, but to me, even when something does not work out, I view it as a learning experience, using it to inform rather than halt future decisions. For example, Kristen, my partner at For Good, and I tried renting out one of the spaces we had for parties and baby showers, because the community was requesting it. But the maintenance and cleaning fees after events soon became unsustainable, and it became clear that we could not both keep it affordable and pay for the upkeep required for frequent use. So instead, we stuck to renting it out to small business owners and hosting our own events for the community.

Early on at the Free Store, too, I once went in to find nine old television sets that I then had to pay to properly dispose of. To some, that may have felt like a confirmation of the concerns people raised when I first started the Free Store—and an example of people taking advantage. But that experience taught me to set clear boundaries and guidelines surrounding what we could or could not accept. Every so-called failure was merely a growing pain; it was a redirection rather than a red light.

Not trying because we are afraid of failing robs us of an opportunity to grow and learn and shuts down the possibility of success. In 2015, for instance, we hosted a gun buyback event at the Free Store. Often, for these sorts of events, people offer gift cards as an incentive in exchange for the guns. But I decided to go a different route. I learned that a local union was struggling to find welders, so rather than a financial incentive, we gave those who came to turn in a gun a token to get a free welding education. Just like when I started the Free Store, naysayers around me told me they did not think anyone would come—that the tokens would not be enough of an incentive. But I went for it. We didn't ask questions about what the person did with the gun. The goal wasn't to check if a crime had been committed with the weapons. What I wanted was to get some weapons off the street and fill a community need at the same time. That day, we collected close to fifty guns. And twenty-two people became full-time welders.

I'm not afraid to fail, nor do I get discouraged when something I try doesn't work. Because in most cases, what we're doing *now* isn't working either. There are other careers, for example, that don't have enough workers and would benefit from expanding their hiring practices to include people who would otherwise be shut out. In Georgia, for example, some fire departments are made up of people who are incarcerated. While I believe that the imprisoned should have agency over the work they do, I believe this shows that those inmates have something to offer. It's important to be creative and try different approaches to remedy our societal issues. You must believe in people and cheer for them. Outcomes aren't always going to be perfect. I have my heart broken a lot. But it comes with the opportunity for something great to happen, too, and that's worth the chance.

Being the First Yes

Though I have never wanted to be a successful businesswoman, because it doesn't bring me joy, I have always loved the idea of helping people get there. A running joke between John and me is that I'm on a mission to find a new job for every member of his staff. I often ask the young people who work for him, "So what do you *really* want to do?" I'm always trying to figure out the area where someone shines, where their skill set would be most useful, what would make them most happy and fulfilled.

I do the same with my volunteers. Rather than expect that they will excel at every task, I take the time to learn about them and find what their thing is. Placing this idea at the center of our organizations, I believe, would both motivate staffers and help our businesses run better.

We have to acknowledge that not everybody is good at

everything, and that just because someone fails in one area does not mean they might not excel in another. It's about harnessing their skill sets and finding the place where they belong. Rather than focusing on businesses, we should focus on people.

When you are in a position of leadership, people are going to come to you with ideas, visions, and dreams. Often, the response many hear is no. *No, this won't work. No, this isn't a good idea. No, I don't think it's right for us.* For me, it's important to be somebody's first yes. I want to be the person who gives people an opportunity—their first client, first investor, first cheerleader. Recently, I met a woman who had worked for a social impact agency for a long time but dreamed of striking out on her own. She liked the work but wanted to have more agency over the clients she worked with, to set her own hours and have more flexibility. I hired her as a fundraiser for Free Store and our umbrella organization, For Good. We were her first solo client, her first yes.

I try to play this role in my personal life as well. Sandra, the Portuguese girl who translated for me in school when I first moved to Harrison, is a teacher in Bloomfield who dreamt of offering individualized tutoring for students who were differently abled. She is an education advocate, and she knew from her experience working in schools that children were getting passed over in traditional classrooms. Every week, she would tell me about her dream and what she envisioned it looking like. I knew she was talented.

When my youngest, August, was learning to read, he at first

struggled a lot. Because I knew how closely tied literacy is to success, it was scary when I did not see him improve. I felt like every day I was trying, and it wasn't clicking for him. So I brought in Sandra, and I loved seeing her do the tutoring work she was so good at. Under her tutelage, August quickly mastered letters and words that I had been trying to teach him for months. This woman was obviously born to do this work.

One day, I asked Sandra, "If you were to set up a specialized tutoring company, what would you name this imaginary business?" When she told me—Essex Literacy Center—I created a logo, Instagram account, and business cards for her.

"Now you have to do it," I told her. Back when I had been dreaming about launching the Free Store, one of the first things I did was mock up a logo. That was the moment my dream felt real. I had to follow through.

Now, I wanted to give Sandra the same push . . . and it worked. She put her ideas into action, launched her tutoring business, and it took off beyond her wildest dreams. Today, she even has a waitlist. Every student she teaches improves dramatically. She just needed someone to say, "I see what you see, too."

I do a lot of panels in which people call me an entrepreneur. That is not how I view myself, but I do feel like I am very good at launching *other* entrepreneurs. *Shark Tank* is so fun because it's gratifying to see people's dreams come true. I remember what it was like to birth the Free Store and have always wanted to help other people take charge of their careers in the same way. Every family has someone who will be the one to break the cycle—whether of poverty, abuse, etc. Every community, including mine, has creativity and imagination. But not all have the help they need to bring those skills to life.

Women in Braddock would often come to me with business ideas, but for a long time, there was little more I could offer these aspiring entrepreneurs beyond advice. I had neither an extensive network nor other resources for them. Moving into a space is the first legitimizing step into a business. But because so much of the town had been abandoned, Braddock did not have a lot of turnkey spaces available for these budding entrepreneurs.

One day, in late 2018, I walked past a building that had a for sale sign. It was an old pharmacy turned plumbing business that had been vacant for years. The exterior was yellow and had a toilet painted on it. When I walked in and saw the layout, I immediately said to myself, *This would be amazing for entrepreneurs.* That same afternoon, by chance, Kristen and I had a meeting scheduled with potential For Good funders. I pitched them my idea: a coworking and incubator space where women entrepreneurs could get start-up support for small businesses. And just like that, the Hollander Project was born.

We named the space after the pharmacy that had stood there decades ago and used the same font and a similar color—a sage green—for the exterior that the legacy business had used. Almost every week, some senior community member comes in and says something like, "Oh my god, I used to come when it was a pharmacy. My mom used to send me to buy cigarettes." Most of the people we hired to do the work were women: the lead contractor, the muralists, the interior decorators. The Hollander has a glass front and the entrepreneurs' information is displayed on the windows. There is a lobby with a couch before you reach the offices the women rent for $150 or less per month—just enough to cover our utilities and maintenance fees. The lots on either side of the building were empty. On one, we created a labyrinth composed of local plants. On the other, we have a huge chess-board, a piano, as well as lounge chairs and umbrellas under which people can gather. People come and take photos of the murals we commissioned for the exterior walls, one of which proudly features the faces of three women. It's a space created for and by women.

The businesses that have been born at the Hollander, which can hold up to thirteen entrepreneurs at a time, run the gamut. A lash artist who did customer data entry at a local hospital was among the first to join us. Like my friend Sandra, she had wanted to start her own business but was too afraid to take the leap. Before the Hollander, she was doing lashes on the side out of her home. She said seeing her name on the door at the Hol-lander made her business feel more real. Now, she's making six figures and started a school to train aspiring lash artists. She was recently able to rent her own space elsewhere and shared on her social media how grateful she was that the Hollander believed in her.

We have a makeup artist and a competitive dance troupe of local girls. We had a woman who was a fashion designer and made prom dresses. We have a personal trainer who is a single mom and recently completed a fundraising campaign to start her own facility. We have a Black mental health therapist who focuses on young people. She's my daughter's therapist, as well, and we adore her. We had a woman who did tattoo removals and offered former gang members and sex trafficking survivors her services for free. She was forced to close her business after being diagnosed with early onset dementia, and her spot went to a women's drug rehabilitation facility.

We have an organization called HOOP, which stands for Helping Out Our People. They have tracked down every family in the district that has lost someone to gun violence and offer the bereaved services like drop-in therapy and trauma yoga. The founders were inspired to start the organization after losing a child to gun violence. Their son, who was sixteen and left behind a twin sister, was at a playground when a thirteen-year-old shot him. I'm a firefighter two blocks away from the Hollander, and it is surreal how full-circle this work is for me. Anytime someone is killed, we are called to wash the blood off the streets. And when I get the call, so does HOOP. That affected family comes to the HOOP office at the Hollander for counseling and support, and the belongings of their loved ones get donated to the Free Store.

When the business owners outgrow us, we bring in someone from the waitlist. The woman entrepreneurs we work with at the Hollander are people who have heard "no" a lot. They are heads of households, single moms—people for whom running their own business has been life-changing. In addition to space for their businesses, we have offered the entrepreneurs and other women in the area free headshots, professional makeovers, tax advice, and help with cover letters. The Hollander has become a makeshift community center. We have held events to facilitate free health care for adults without insurance and even for their pets. Every month, we give away $250 mini grants to help families make ends meet, and we do not monitor how that money is spent. We keep trying different things and seeing what makes an impact.

The Hollander has allowed us to be the first yes for dozens of people. And I believe that first acknowledgment stays with people. You don't forget your first yes. You don't forget the people who listened to you or took a chance on you. Just as was the case when I was trying to start the Free Store, many people's first instinct is to shut others down. We tend to hear no the most, and that tends to be what our brains remember. Rather than any positive feedback, we play on a loop the negative voice that tells us we won't succeed. I urge us all to try to be that first yes; to be the person who tells others that their dreams are valid, that they can do it, and that we are here to help.

CHAPTER 9

A TENDER FUTURE

n the fall of 2024, soon after school started, my son August had his first soccer game of the season. Out of all my children, August is probably the child who most takes after me. He is sweet, earnest, and sensitive; a happy-go-lucky kid who always has a smile on his face. He's a helper and a team player. Always wants to make sure everyone is included. August loves life and is always in a good mood. Before the game, he kept telling me how excited he was. He was just starting fifth grade, and the team he was playing against was made up of much taller middle school kids who were a bit older than he was. August's team lost the game, but that is not why he ended up leaving the game upset.

The kids on the opposing team were being bullies. Every time they scored, they would point to August and his teammates and laugh. They taunted them at every opportunity, and one told August, "You're useless." The team had worked so hard to prepare for the game, and it was awful and heart-wrenching to watch their efforts be ridiculed and their first experience on the field be ruined. The situation was concerning enough that several parents reached out to the school afterward to complain.

In the car on the way home, August told me he just couldn't understand how they could be so mean. "Mom, I felt so confident going into it," he said. "I never want to play soccer again." His spirit had been broken.

"No, we're not going to let these mean kids win," I responded. "I'm so sorry you're hurting. I wish I could change that, but there are going to be mean people. That's just part of life. All you can do is not be one of them."

One of the hardest parts of being a parent is seeing your kid get hurt and not being able to do anything to help. What I realized watching that game, and what I told August, is that mean kids become mean parents, and then they have mean kids. It's a cycle that continues until someone decides to behave differently. There were some parents on the sidelines who were mirroring the kids' behavior, yelling and fighting with the referees. It always baffles me when parents get so invested, especially at that age, when the stakes are so low. I thought in my head, *None of our kids are that good! I just wanted both teams to have fun.*

Had one of my older kids been in this situation, they probably would have stood up for themselves or cussed out the other team members. But August isn't like that. That doesn't exist within him. He often reminds me of how gentle children can be before social conditioning kicks in.

All my kids carry different tiers of sensibility and sensitivity, and I hope we've fostered an environment in which they can feel safe to wholly be themselves. When our oldest, Karl, was younger, John and I were hosting a wedding between two men at the house. Same-sex marriage was not yet legal at that point, but there was a rogue judge who issued marriage licenses in brave defiance of the law, and we sometimes hosted these weddings at our house. There was still a sense of novelty and excitement surrounding the possibility of this sort of union. On the day of the ceremony, I was getting nervous and rushing to buy the last few things I needed and decorate the house.

Karl came up to me and, sensing my anxious excitement, said, "Dad marries people all the time. What's the big deal?" I told him that we were making a bit more of a fuss because it was two boys who were getting married this time.

"And?" he responded. He could not comprehend. It was a reminder that kids are free of hate until someone teaches it to them.

Raising three kids who are very different has forced me to reckon with how I see and approach the world and what core values I want to pass on to them. My oldest is serious and responsible. He started working the day he turned fifteen and saves money without having to be told. I joke that he probably has a 401(k) that I don't know about.

My daughter, Grace, challenges me; she likes dark humor and is very cool. Her first word was "no." One of her favorite shows is *Arrested Development*, which we sometimes watch together. By the time she was in kindergarten, she told us she wanted to shave a skull outline onto the side of her head. (We were at the hair salon the next day.) She always loved Halloween and gravitated toward ghosts and witches.

With all my kids, I try not to "right fight," meaning that I don't argue my point of view or prioritize them agreeing with me. I try to meet them where they are. I don't push too much, because my job is not to make them feel embarrassed or ashamed for what they might think or feel. I give them dignity and appropriate autonomy. Now that my daughter is a teenager, she has become moodier and more dramatic. She changes her mind a lot and has become more stubborn. These are all traits I want her to have when she goes out into the world, even if it is sometimes difficult and not so fun when directed at me. With Grace, who is a bit more anxious than my other kids, I make sure she has the tools that she needs when I'm not the person she wants to talk to. My role is to facilitate rather than dictate their development.

Give Yourself Grace

When my oldest was younger, he slept over at a friend's house. He came home and said, "Mom, can you believe that their mom cooks dinner for them every day?" There was a time when my child just innocently pointing that out might have made me feel inadequate.

But rather than feel bad, I simply responded, "That's nice, but that's not realistic for every family. I'm glad that works for their family, but I'm not a good cook. And I travel and work a lot." I embrace being an imperfect parent. I don't cook dinner most nights. I'm sometimes late to soccer because I go to the wrong field. A few times, I thought they had school when they didn't and did not realize until we were halfway out the door. I do not obsess over perfect attendance and let the kids miss school if that is what they need that day. In all cases, the world did not end.

The stress of parents right now is a national concern. In August 2024, Dr. Vivek H. Murthy, the U.S. surgeon general, released a thirty-five-page report called *Parents Under Pressure* on the immense stress that parents are facing today. According to the report, 40 percent of parents in the United States say "they are so stressed they cannot function." Researchers said that this is the result of the pressure parents feel to exert all possible resources to enrich their children's lives and equip them to thrive in the modern economy. Dr. Murthy also called out an "intensifying culture of comparison" exacerbated by unrealistic standards set by social media influencers and trends. "Chasing these unreasonable expectations has left many families feeling exhausted, burned out, and perpetually behind," he writes.

To put it more plainly: We are all striving to be perfect, and it is making us sick. More than ever before, modern parents are committed to doing the most to offer their kids every single opportunity and advantage within their reach, especially if it is one they did not have. It is natural to want to improve our children's lives and set them up well for the future, but this fixation has reached chronic levels. We are chasing an impossible standard that no one will ever meet.

I learned early in my parenting journey that there is no such thing as a perfect parent. As I have settled into motherhood, I have learned to double down on what is important to me and let go of the rest. I joke that when I had my first child, every time he dropped his pacifier, I would wash it thoroughly, but by the third, I was taking it out of the dog's mouth. There is a freedom in leaving room for our own flawed humanity within motherhood. And in setting our own standard rather than letting others—be they family, bloggers, or friends—determine how we approach parenting. It is hard enough without this added pressure to conform.

It is inevitable that we will disappoint others in our approach, sometimes even our children. Everyone has their own set of values, and these will not always align with what is within your reach. I don't set unrealistic expectations on other people, and I don't set them for myself either. I acknowledge that I am a person who has had trauma and is going to make mistakes and perhaps fall short in some ways. A daily home-cooked dinner is not something that I will likely ever offer my children. I do not keep every napkin with their scribbles or artwork they make at school like my mom and grandmother did. But I will do arts and crafts with them and go to their games. I will support their interests and give them freedom to explore their passions. To me, that is just as important.

Instead of aiming for perfection and overexerting myself, I aim for balance. My number one priority is that my kids feel loved. Growing up, though my mom worked a ton and we lived in different homes, my stability came from the love she and my grandmother offered in abundance. Knowing you're loved and supported goes a long way, and it's what I offer to my children unconditionally. I remind them often.

When they make a request that I can't fulfill: "I can't right now. Love you!"

When I drop them off at school: "Have a good day. Love you!"

Once, when my son was eight, he was performing at a school concert when I yelled out, "I love you, August!" from the audience. He was mortified, and the next time he had a show, he told me, "Mom, don't yell anything embarrassing!" But I need them to hear it until it seeps into their bones. I want it to be the foundation they lie on, the great stabilizing force of their lives. They are loved. They are cherished. That will never change.

Love is a transformative force with the potential to transform individual lives and collective communities. Few receive love in its totality, as defined by bell hooks, getting piecemeal versions while lacking the rest. In reflecting on her description of love, I am reminded of my own childhood. There was care, of course—the peeled grapes, the walks hand in hand, the gentle touch—but what made their love so impactful was that it was layered and grounded. It was expansive and safe. It helped me stand on my own two feet.

Love is at the center of and the driving force toward self-acceptance, healthy relationships, and social change. Children who are loved become adults who have a capacity for love. In thinking about how to actively love my kids, I return to my commitment to prepare them to be agents of change in the world and to stand firm in their values and worth. I am raising them to be themselves.

Whenever my kids complain to me about a part of their upbringing that they wish would change, I use it as an opportunity to help them solidify their own values. They hate taking the bus home, for example. It's a long and stuffy ride made longer by the inconsistent air-conditioning. But while some days I can pick them up, other days it's just not possible. They sometimes get upset about that. What I tell them is that if there's something they didn't like or find fault with, perhaps it is a need they can prioritize for themselves in their future. If they wish they could eat more home-cooked meals, maybe they could take cooking lessons or marry a partner who loves to cook. If they don't like taking the bus to school, perhaps they can find a school for their future children that's close to their home. As parents, we can only do the best we can, and when it's our kids' turn, they can do their best, too—whatever that looks like for them. As much as we give our kids grace, we also need to have grace with ourselves. My kids may be frustrated in the moment, but our foundation is never shaken.

Teach Empathy

There was a time when I was not sure I would have biological children. Volunteer work I had done with kids—with a group that helped children born addicted to drugs, as well as with organizations trying to recruit foster parents—had made me unsure. Aside from being terrified of birth, I knew there were many kids out there in need. I reasoned that there were lots of places where I could put my energy instead of bringing a new person into this world. At times, the disparity between my children's lives and that of other children I had encountered is still jarring. Here I was monitoring their salt intake when there were babies who were totally alone in the world.

In 2022, I started visiting a trauma-centered preschool in Pittsburgh once a week. All the kids who attend are in foster care after having been removed from their parents' home by the state, and many have experienced some form of extreme trauma, like sexual or physical abuse. The teachers are specifically trained to handle the challenges these kids might face. If a kid cries for hours straight or lashes out, they are trained in how to soothe them. These behaviors are rarely a result of the situation at hand, but rather the bubbling up of a deeper pain. It's the sort of intervention that would be life-changing if applied widely, not only to children who have been harmed, but to all children.

It is important to me that my kids be able to recognize the root of their own behavior. I often think back to something Mr. Rogers said in a Senate hearing meant to decide whether to slash federal funding for public education television. "I feel that if we in public television can only make it clear that feelings are mentionable and manageable, we will have done a great service for mental health," he said. He described his show as a "meaningful expression of care" for children and added that he felt showing that "two men could be working out their feelings of anger" was "much more dramatic than showing something of gunfire."

By now, it must be clear that I'm inclined to agree. Mine is a therapy-happy home where both kids and adults are encouraged to explore and talk about their feelings. Grace has always been more anxious and nervous than my other kids, so early on I brought her to someone who could help her cope with those emotions. Being in the public eye, I take extra care to make politics a small part of their world. I want it to be an afterthought in their life, though sometimes it's an unavoidable consideration—like when I was thinking of visiting Brazil in fall 2024 when my father's health was declining. I had started to think about how to keep the kids safe there when my father passed away. My daughter and oldest son often say they don't want to go places where there will be a lot of people who might know me or their dad. When their dad was sick, people would often come up to them to ask how he was doing. It was out of kindness, but the kids would sometimes get annoyed. I never pushed them to answer. "Just because someone asks you a question doesn't mean you owe them an answer—especially if it makes you uncomfortable," I told them. They're in a stage in which they are struggling for and craving autonomy.

Still, I often tell them stories about my childhood and remind them of all the privileges they enjoy. Not to make them feel bad but so they know that it's important to be grateful. To take the good when you have it and receive it in the best way possible. Parents have to be like a hammer when it comes to the messages we want our children to receive. They have to hear these things so much until it becomes normal—like reminding them about their posture. I have a friend whose daughter is neurodivergent. A lot of kids avoid her and don't want to be friends with her, because she comes off as too enthusiastic. Driving back home from school one day, I asked the kids to go out of their way to find and connect with her. Everything matters—what you do and don't do. What you give and take away. How you treat other people not only impacts that person but everyone with whom they come in contact. You have the power to help someone have a great day or a bad day. You have that power.

Tell the Truth

Once, after Karl came home from a sleepover, he jumped in the car and shared that his friend's parents were getting divorced. The friend was devastated, he said.

"Would you and Dad ever get divorced?" he asked. John and I responded at the same time from the front seat.

"No," said John.

"Maybe," I responded. John was, understandably, surprised by my response. But I explained that, though I loved him and hoped we'd always be together, I wanted to be realistic and honest with the kids about all of life's possibilities.

I am not the mom who is going to lie to her kids. Divorce can be a devastating experience for any family, of course. There are a lot of adjustments that need to be made, and for kids it can feel like a seismic shift. But I do not want my kids to feel that their world will end if their parents are not together. Instead, I want them to know that marriage is fine while it works and that it's also fine when it ends. My family is very pro-divorce when it is needed. I'm grateful I got to see my mom make the decision to leave her marriage when it was probably harder than staying. That I got to see both her and my dad happier apart. Growing up, I would see friends' parents in unhealthy situations who would stay together because that's just what you do. Because they had seen their parents stick it out and therefore firmly believed they had to do the same; that they were in this for life. But for me, my mother's divorce made it so that I did not grow up in a home in which there was arguing or fighting. I wanted the kids to know that different types of family were not lesser than and could also be joyful. And I also wanted to send the message that they were free to change their minds. None of us are tied to one decision or another if it makes us unhappy.

I do not believe in placating your kids. Being gentle, to me, does not mean coddling them or sheltering them from the realities of what could happen. It means preparing them for any possibility. When John had the stroke, the kids naturally had questions. The biggest one was, "Is Dad going to die?" At the time, I told them the truth: that I did not know. "I don't know that answer, but whatever happens, we're going to make it through together," I said. When I get called out to a fire, I leave a radio at the house so they can listen in to what's happening. Sometimes, if it's a particularly dangerous call, they're too scared to listen. But they know they always have the option. Giving kids the truth is a gift. The truth can be comforting.

You Can Always Start Over
(and Sometimes You Must)

Perhaps some might disagree with how I choose to answer my children's questions, and it's understandable. But it's important to me that my kids have the truths they need to make informed decisions. Every day they wake up is an opportunity for a brand-new experience. My mother is a wonderful teacher in this regard. She has been religiously studying Italian on Duolingo for years and says that, when she's ready, she plans to move there. When I say, "Mom, but you're seventy!" she responds, "So what?" There is no age limit for dreaming or imagining a new life for yourself. Likewise, I want my kids to know that they can change their minds whenever they feel unhappy, and no prescribed social expectation should hold them back. I always tell them, "You have to be flexible. The trees with branches that can bend don't break on a windy day." We often have no control over what happens to us, and life can change in a second. Nothing stays as it is now, and it shouldn't. All we *can* control is our responses when faced with difficult situations.

In my own life, I am oriented toward action, toward focusing on the things over which I have some influence. The kids complain a lot about the uniforms they are required to wear. Or argue that school should be four days a week instead of five. My rule is, if this is something that you can change, work on it. But if not, then you must change your relationship with it. If there's a product you don't like, can you make something better? Do you want to lobby the education department and petition for a four-day school week? No? Then you have to come to terms with your reality. There are things in our control and so many that aren't. To complain about something you cannot or will not make an effort to change is a waste of energy.

I do not harbor grand ambitions for what my children's future will look like, but I do have hopes for how they will move through the world and the values they will carry with them. "Raising a child requires profound strength and hope," writes Angela Garbes in *Essential Labor*, in which she presents a radical new vision for motherhood. "You must believe in your ability to forge a future that is better than the present we currently inhabit, even if you never live to see it." As much as I hope to see a tender world in my lifetime, and will continue to work toward it, my children are the next link in the chain that will guide us there. My job is to instill in them the values that will make them adults who can and are willing to participate in the creation of a more tender, loving society, however that work looks for them. One day, they will not be under my care; it is an inevitability and not something I lament. I am not one of those mothers who hopes my children will stay young forever, because I know I am not raising them for me, but for the world. If I have done my job well, they will leave my home with the tools to make good decisions when I am not there to guide them. Kindness, flexibility, and grace are my guiding principles, and these are the driving force behind all my decisions as a parent. My hope is that they will be able to both face the world as it is and become catalysts for change, with the freedom and foresight to envision what the world could become.

Embracing the Tenderness Within Us

When children are born, doctors and parents wait in anticipation for the first cry—a signal of health and life. The first time we open our mouths and make our voices heard, shout out to the world, our parents understand that we are strong and ready to withstand this new environment. Slowly, we are stripped of this essential right and visceral need. We grow up and start by pointing around us and asking what, what, what, and then move on to why. *Why is the sky blue? Why do I have to brush my teeth? Why does only Mom cook? Why can only girls wear skirts?* That is when the silencing begins. We start to receive the lessons that alert us to the social order, to how things have always been, and to how we are meant to behave or conform. Children are admonished for speaking up or expressing pain, frustration, anger, or sadness. For too long, what we have been taught is not tenderness and love but assimilation. We are meant to be quiet and absorb or accept the world's injustices. For women and people of color, in particular, expressions of vulnerability can lead to further marginalization or misunderstanding. The fear that we will be ridiculed, shamed, or quieted keeps us in a state of resigned or resentful acceptance of whatever the world throws at us.

But it is time we reclaim the child we lost along the way—the tenderness, the curiosity, the awe. What's beautiful about children is that, in their eyes, the world is a malleable place. Nothing is fixed and anything is possible. Giving space to our inner child means continuing to question and probe at what we are told cannot be changed. Do not believe the lies. Do not believe that this is the only way, that you must change while the world remains the same. Every generation, we see immense movement in our social values. Advancements we did not think were possible have come to be. We can do more. We can strike at the very core of a society that pushes toughness and insist on tenderness—from our friends, our coworkers, our family, and our leaders.

Not everyone will be ready to make the shift. But start with yourself. Give yourself that gift. Believe, deep inside, that you are not too much, too emotional, or too soft. It is more convenient for others to tell those of us who move through the world prioritizing kindness and gentleness that we are in the wrong. Shifting the responsibility onto those who are brave enough to sit in hard feelings releases others from having to do the work themselves. But think how much better the world would be if we tried to lead with a velvet rather than an iron glove. Think of how much safer we stand to feel. Strength does not come from perpetuating or ignoring injustice. It comes from accepting and being with big feelings and then pushing forward. From developing resilience by letting in the pain and overcoming it. Do not fight the tears. But also, do not stay there. Crying is not the destination, but it is where we start.

ACKNOWLEDGMENTS

I owe an extraordinary debt to my mother, Ester, and my grandmother, Teresinha (Bibi). More than for my accomplishments, I want to be known for being their daughter and granddaughter.

My partner, John; my children, Karl, Grace, and August; and my pets, Levi, Artie, and Potato: It has been a great honor to love and be loved by you. May the whole world know such love.

To Karl and Susan, too: Thank you for making me feel loved and accepted, always. Everyone deserves to be loved exactly as they are.

To my Free Store family: I'm inspired by your kindness, generosity, and commitment to serving our community. Thank you.

Thank you to Jennifer Rohrer and Georgia Bodnar for seeing something beyond the tears. To Christy Fletcher for seeing this book across the finish line and to Laurie-Maude Chenard for her edits and support. Thank you to the entire Putnam team, especially to Michelle Howry and Ashley Di Dio. You are as kind as you are talented.

And Concepción de León—how lucky was I to have my first book experience be with such an amazing collaborator. I am grateful for our connection, and I will miss all our time together.

The world is a better place because of the soft people in it. We can only be as strong as we are soft, and I am grateful for those who have shown me that path. May we all keep our hearts soft enough to keep breaking.

Adult Children of Emotionally Immature Parents: How to Heal from Distant, Rejecting, or Self-Involved Parents by Lindsay C. Gibson, PsyD

All About Love by bell hooks

The Body Keeps the Score: Brain, Mind, and Body in the Healing of Trauma by Bessel van der Kolk, MD

Break the Cycle: A Guide to Healing Intergenerational Trauma by Dr. Mariel Buqué

Essential Labor: Mothering as Social Change by Angela Garbes

The Highly Sensitive Person: How to Thrive When the World Overwhelms You by Elaine N. Aron, PhD

My Grandmother's Hands: Racialized Trauma and the Pathway to Mending Our Hearts and Bodies by Resmaa Menakem, MSW, LICSW, SEP

The Myth of Normal: Trauma, Illness, and Healing in a Toxic Culture by Gabor Maté, MD, with Daniel Maté

Radical Belonging: How to Survive and Thrive in an Unjust World (While Transforming It for the Better) by Lindo Bacon, PhD

Radical Compassion: Learning to Love Yourself and Your World with the Practice of RAIN by Tara Brach

Widen the Window: Training Your Brain and Body to Thrive During Stress and Recover from Trauma by Elizabeth A. Stanley, PhD

50 **workplaces can be hostile spaces:** LeanIn.Org and McKinsey & Company, *Women in the Workplace 2023*, https://www.mckinsey.com /featured-insights/diversity-and-inclusion/women-in-the-workplace -2023.

51 **displaying so-called feminine traits:** Jennifer L. Berdahl et al., "Work as a Masculinity Contest," *Journal of Social Issues* 74, no. 3 (September 2018), https://spssi.onlinelibrary.wiley.com/doi/full/10.1111/josi.12289.

56 **before the Prudential Center was built:** New Jersey Economic Development Authority, "NJEDA Releases Draft List of NJ Food Desert Communities for Public Input," press release, January 4, 2022, https:// www.njeda.gov/njeda-releases-draft-list-of-nj-food-desert-communi ties-for-public-input.

57 **One participant who had tried:** Gabriela Dory et al., "A Phenomenological Understanding of Residents' Emotional Distress of Living in an Environmental Justice Community," *International Journal of Qualitative Studies in Health and Well-Being* 12, no. 1 (January 5, 2017), https://pmc.ncbi.nlm.nih.gov/articles/PMC5328345.

62 **In poor communities of color:** Tina Rosenberg, "Fighting Street Gun Violence as if It Were a Contagion, *The New York Times*, May 8, 2018, https://www.nytimes.com/2018/05/08/opinion/fighting-street-gun -violence-as-if-it-were-a-contagion.html.

95 **Garbes alludes to this:** Asma Khalid, Sylvie Douglis, and Michelle Aslam, "Raising Kids Is Hard Work. The Way We Think About It Can Shift How We Value Mothering," *Life Kit* (podcast), NPR, May 16, 2022.

115 **Discussing "healthy anger":** Tara Brach, *Radical Compassion: Learning to Love Yourself and Your World with the Practice of RAIN* (Penguin, 2019).

147 **advocating for a delight practice:** Catherine Price, "When the World Feels Dark, Seek Out Delight," *The New York Times*, December 31, 2023, https://www.nytimes.com/2023/12/31/opinion/delights-connections-mood-health.html.

159 **Rebecca Traister, a political reporter:** Rebecca Traister, "The Vulnerability of John Fetterman," *New York*, October 10, 2022, https://nymag.com/intelligencer/article/john-fetterman-dr-oz-pennsylvania-senate-race.html.

INDEX

ABIN, 139
acceptability, lens of, 83
accountability, lack of, 44
addiction, 86, 137, 178–79
ADHD, 138, 164
adults, children versus, 81–82, 85
affirmations, 100–101
Air Force One, 171–72
alcohol dependency, 178
Aldi, 116–17
And His Lovely Wife (Schultz), 157
anger
    healthy, 115–16
    metabolizing, 114–19
Ann Taylor, 103
anti-abortion protesters, 42–43
Aron, Elaine N., 155, 164
Arrested Development, 193
Artie (dog), 145–46
arts
    beautification projects, 99–101
    emphasis on, 70–71, 100
    murals, 100
assassinations, 33
assumptions/questions, inappropriate,
    112–15
auditory processing disorder, 158

baby cuddler, work as, 67
Bacon, Lindo, 116, 124
Ban the Box legislation, 180–81

Banana Republic, 103
Barnhill, Mrs., 18–19, 20, 103
beautification projects, 99–101
behavior, genes and, 77–78
Bibi
    author's recollections of, 17–18
    care from, 22–23
    childhood of, 35
    as "cycle breaker," 35–36
    death of, 38, 144–45, 147
    immigration and, 11–12
    immigration status and, 22
    life experiences of, 38–39
    pandemic and, 139
    Telmo and, 140
Biden, Jill, 162
Biden, Joe, 151, 171–72
Big Brothers Big Sisters of America,
    54, 66, 77
book event, 111–12
Book of Delights, The (Gay), 147
boundaries, 94, 96, 126
Brach, Tara, 115, 116
Braddock, Pennsylvania. *See also*
    individual people and
    businesses
    article on, 70–72
    author's move to, 78–79, 84
    author's visit to, 72–76
    beautification projects in, 99–101
    commercial spaces in, 186

Braddock, Pennsylvania (*cont*)
  John's role in, 96–97
  social community of, 87–89, 107
Braddock Carnegie Library, 88
Braddock Tigers, 111
"Braddock's World-Famous
    Sunflowers," 108
brand ambassador, author as, 44, 47
Brazil
  author's childhood in, 13
  author's departure from, 11–12
  crime in, 26–27
Brazilian Carnival event, 133–34
Brazilian way (*jeitinho brasileiro*),
    169–70
Break the Cycle (Buqué), 35
Brooklyn Bridge, 72
Brown, Sherrod, 157
Build-a-Bear unicorn, 168
Buqué, Mariel, 35–36
Burnham, Terry, 77–78
burnout, 86

cafuné, 37
car dealership, as home, 109–10
cardiomyopathy, 150
care/care work. *See also* Bibi;
    parenting/mothering
  devaluation of, 95
  emergency childcare, 98–99
  exchange of, 94–95
  intergenerational, 11, 19, 89
  sharing load of, 96
Carnegie, Andrew, 70, 88
Carnegie Foundation, 88
Carnegie libraries, 88
Carnegie Mellon University, 88
Carrey, Jim, 83
Caste (Wilkerson), 55–56

Center for American Progress, 143
Centers for Disease Control and
    Prevention, 163
change
  burden of, 32–33
  difficult nature of, 78
childcare, emergency, 98–99
children
  adults versus, 81–82
  August, 109, 139, 145, 162,
    184–85, 191–92, 197
  Grace, 101, 152–55, 156, 193,
    194, 199–200
  Karl, 91–92, 161, 193, 194,
    200, 201
children, adults versus, 81–82, 85
clean pain, 60
Clemmons, Officer, 34
Coats disease, 153, 154
collaboration, 66
Columbia Teachers College, 47
communal responsibility, 70–71
community. *See also* Braddock,
    Pennsylvania; *individual people*
  safety practitioners in, 60–61
  support from, 13–14
comparison, culture of, 195
compassion, lens of, 75
Costa Rica, yoga retreat in,
    70, 84
Cottom, Tressie McMillan, 118
COVID-19 pandemic
  Bibi's death and, 38, 145
  changes after, 110
  immigrants and, 143
  life during, 136–42, 148, 169
  parenting during, 95
  pool closure during, 133
  verbal attack during, 116–17

crisis nursery, 98–99
criticism
    directed at author, 2–3
    overcoming, 3
crying. *See also* feelings/emotions
    author's discussion of, 4
    as moment of silence, 120
    as strength, 8
    suppression of, 7–8, 30–31
Cure Violence Global, 61
cycle breakers, 35–36

DACA (Deferred Action for
    Childhood Arrivals), 141–42
Dartmouth College, Rogers's
    speech at, 36
death, joy and, 147
defensiveness, as learned protective
    mechanism, 57–58, 59–60
Deferred Action for Childhood
    Arrivals (DACA), 141–42
delight, joy and, 146–48
deportation, 24–25, 26. *See also*
    immigrants/immigration
depression, 161–63. *See also* mental
    health
Destinee, 54–55, 66, 76
detachment, 123
difficult people, approach to,
    85–86, 125
dirty pain, 60
disagreements, as natural, 90
divorce, possibility of, 201
dogs
    Artie, 145–46
    Levi, 139, 145
    medical experiments and, 152
do-it-yourself projects, 70
Dreamers, 141–42

drug use, increase in, 137. *See also*
    substance use
drug withdrawal, newborns and, 67

Edgar Thomson Steel Works, 110
elopement, 80
embarrassment, 120
emotional trauma, 35–36
emotions/feelings
    anger, 114–19
    author's experience expressing, 3–4
    crying and, 4, 7–8, 30–31, 120
    expressing as strength, 7
    finding home for, 30–39
    of hatred, 117–19, 120–21
    importance of, 82
    joy and delight, 146–48
    love, 124–25, 196–97
    shame, 118, 120, 123
    silencing, 23–30
    suppression of, 62
    unconditional love, 124
empathy
    disconnecting from others' actions
        and, 126
    Free Store and, 177
    healing hurt with, 61
    lack of, 48
    living life out loud and, 164
    teaching, 198–201
entrepreneurs, in Braddock, 186–89
epigenetics, 35
Essential Labor (Garbes), 95, 204
Essex Literacy Center, 185
experimental urbanism, 70–71

failure
    embracing, 181–83
    fear of, 68–69

Faxina, 38
fear of failure, 68–69
feelings/emotions
    anger, 114–19
    author's experience expressing, 3–4
    crying and, 4, 7–8, 30–31, 120
    expressing as strength, 7
    finding home for, 30–39
    of hatred, 117–19, 120–21
    importance of, 82
    joy and delight, 146–48
    love, 124–25, 196–97
    shame, 118, 120, 123
    silencing, 23–30
    suppression of, 62
    unconditional love, 124
feminine traits, devaluing of, 51
Fetterman, August
    birth of, 109
    love to/from, 145, 197
    in Niagara Falls, 162
    during pandemic, 139
    reading and, 184–85
    soccer game and, 191–92
Fetterman, Grace
    anxiety and, 194, 199–200
    birth of, 101
    Coats disease and, 152–55, 156
    personality of, 193
Fetterman, John
    article on, 70–71
    beautification projects and, 100
    Brazilian Carnival event and,
        133–34
    criticism and, 2–3
    daughter's eye condition and, 153
    developing relationship with,
        74–80
    first meeting with, 73

health of, 149–51, 155–56, 157–59,
        200, 202
    as host of social events, 110
    as lieutenant governor, 129, 131,
        132–33, 149
    as mayor, 70–71, 73, 97, 110, 129
    mental health of, 160–64
    Ms. Phyllis and, 89
    on possibility of divorce, 201
    Senate campaign of, 144, 149, 151,
        156–57, 158–59, 160–61, 171
    shipping container and, 102
    staff of, 183
    youth/senior program and, 101
Fetterman, Karl
    birth of, 91–92
    divorce question from, 201
    John's health and, 161
    parenting/mothering and, 194
    recognition and, 200
    same-sex marriage and, 193
fights, author and, 28
financial auditing, 48, 66, 69, 175
fire academy, 165–68
fire detectors, 103–4
First Amendment, 134
Fisher, Lawrence, 111
food deserts, 57, 69. *See also*
        nutritional education
food insecurity, 67
food stamps, 57, 67
food waste, 104–5
For Good, 181, 184, 186
Fort Indiantown Gap, 131
412 Food Rescue, 105
Free Store 15104
    challenging emergency calls
        and, 166
    conflicts at, 177–78

culture at, 175–76, 179
death of volunteer with, 105–6
difficult people and, 120–21,
    125–26, 136
failure and, 181–82
fundraiser for, 184
importance of, 136
juggling work of, 134, 139, 144
logo for, 185
loss and, 172–73, 188
pandemic and, 137
purpose of, 104, 174–75
start of, 102–3
volunteers with, 105–6, 107
freelance work, 69
furniture, discarded, 16

Garbes, Angela, 95–96, 204
Gay, Ross, 146–47
GED program, 70, 75
genes, behavior and, 77–78
ghost murals, 100
Giovanni, Nikki, 8
grief, 145–46
gun buyback event, 182
gun violence, 61–62, 70, 188

Habitat for Humanity, 66–67
Hanks, Tom, 119
Hardy, John, 61
Harrisburg School District, 132
hatred, demonstrations of,
    117–19, 120–21. *See also*
    microaggressions
healthy anger, 115–16
hedgehogs (prickly people), 85–86
help
    accepting, 96
    reluctance to accept, 92–94

Highly Sensitive Person, The (Aron),
    155, 164
hitchhikers, 42
Hollander Project, 186–89
hooks, bell, 124, 197
HOOP (Helping Out Our
    People), 188
house purchase, 52–53, 66
housing insecurity, 98
human motivation, theory of, 28–29
Hurston, Zora Neale, 136

"I Married My Mother" (Giovanni), 8
IKEA, 103
imagination, 81, 82
immigrants/immigration
    aggression due to, 120–21
    author's, 11–16, 20–21
    Congressional hearings on, 143
    deportation and, 24–25, 26
    pandemic and, 141–42
    political rhetoric regarding, 143–44
    steel industry and, 110
immigration status
    author's, 2–3, 25
    inappropriate comments regarding,
        135–36
    mother's, 29
    permanent resident status and, 48
    as source of danger, 45
imposter syndrome, 136
incarceration, moving on after, 173,
    179–81, 183
injury, response to, 122
inner voice, listening to, 83–84
Institute of Integrative Nutrition, 47
interdependence, 96
intergenerational care, 11, 19, 89.
    See also Bibi

intergenerational trauma, 35–36.
   See also trauma
intuition, listening to, 83–84, 85–86
invisibility, 24
Ironbound, 57

Jawetz, Tom, 142–43
jeitinho brasileiro, 169–70
Jeremiah's Place, 98–99
Jersey Cares, 67
joy and delight, 146–48
"Just Like Me" game, 177

Kean University, 46
Kennedy, Bobby, 33
Key Food, 104
King, Martin Luther, Jr., 33
King, Ruth, 116
Know the Glow, 153
Kristen, 181, 186

lash artist, 187
LeanIn.Org, 50
letter writing, 72
Levi (dog), 139, 145
Lieutenant Governor's Residence, 131
Little Prince, The (Saint-Exupéry),
   81–82, 84–85, 87
localized action, 106–7
loss, 81
love
   hooks on, 124–25, 197
   parenting and, 196–97
   unconditional, 124
Lucido Johnson, Sophie, 93

Madix, Ariana, 171
Maharishi University of
   Management, 83

makeup, helping woman with, 146
Mamãe (author's mother)
   "be invisible" message from, 24
   citizenship and, 142
   as "cycle breaker," 35–36
   divorce of, 202
   exploration of city with, 15–16
   immigration and, 11–14, 23–24,
      25, 27, 88
   immigration status and, 29
   Italian and, 203
   as lifeline, 96
   love from, 37, 196
   memories of Brazil and, 26
   move to New Jersey and, 16–17
   in Newark, 52
   nutritional education and, 46
   second marriage of, 34
   toughness and, 31–32
   treatment of, 15, 34–35, 130, 135
   values of, 21, 159
   verbal attack during call with,
      120–21
Maple Way, 138–39
marathon, 65
Markle, Meghan, 162
marriage proposal, 80
Maslow, Abraham, 28–29
Maté, Gabor, 31, 49–50, 121
McKinsey & Company, 50
Me Too, 49
Mean Genes (Burnham and Phelan),
   77–78
medical care, 97
Menakem, Resmaa, 59, 60
mental health, 160–64, 199
meringues, 145
microaggressions, 50–51, 115, 120.
   See also hatred, demonstrations of

mini grants, 189
Mister Rogers' Neighborhood, 33–34
More Greens, 67–68, 73
Morrison, Toni, 122
mothering/parenting, 95, 191–206.
    See also care/care work
murals, in Braddock, 100
Murthy, Vivek H., 195
My Grandmother's Hands
    (Menakem), 59
Myth of Normal, The (Maté), 31,
    49–50

Narcan, 104, 110, 137. *See also*
    substance use
neurodivergence, 200–201
New Jersey, author's childhood in,
    16–20
New Orleans, Latino family in, 21
New York magazine, 159
New York Times, The, 61–62, 118,
    147–48
Newark, New Jersey
    author in, 36, 46, 52, 79
    Braddock compared to, 72
    description of, 53–54, 56–57
    disparity in, 55
    house fire in, 103
    John's visit to, 76
    nutritional education work in,
        67–68
Niagara Falls, 162
niceness, suspicion of, 58
Nichols, Greg, 111
nonprofit work, 67–69
normalcy, so-called, 31
nutritional education, 46–47, 67–68,
    69. See also *entries beginning
    with "food"*

Obama, Barack, 170
office environment, 48–49,
    50–52
On Being (podcast), 147
online presence, 2–3
overdoses, 104, 137. *See also*
    substance use
Oz, Mehmet, 151, 152,
    158–59, 160

pain, clean versus dirty, 60
pandemic
    Bibi's death and, 38, 145
    changes after, 110
    immigrants and, 143
    life during, 136–42, 148, 169
    parenting during, 95
    pool closure during, 133
    verbal attack during, 116–17
parenting/mothering, 95, 191–206.
    See also care/care work
Parents Under Pressure report, 195
permanent resident status, 48
personal protective equipment, 141
Phelan, Jay, 77–78
Phyllis, Ms., 89–90, 91, 104
pollution, effects of living with, 57
pound cake incident, 76–77
Power of Fun, The (Price), 148
present, living in, 155–56
Price, Catherine, 148
prisons, 180. *See also* incarceration,
    moving on after
Prudential Center, 56
public pools, 132
public service, 65–67, 91, 92–93,
    166–67
public television, 199
Puerto Rico, disparagement of, 143

questions/assumptions, inappropriate, 112–15

racial disparity, 55–56
racial slurs directed at author, 117–19
racism, Morrison on, 122
Radical Belonging (Bacon), 116, 124
Radical Compassion (Brach), 115
ReadyMade, 70–71
refusing to engage, 117–19
rejection, 123–24
resilience, 1, 60
respectability politics, 135
restoration, lens of, 75
Rivers Edge 113 Volunteer Fire Department, 165
Rogers, Fred, 33–34, 35, 36, 71, 199
Rogers, Joanne, 35
Ryan, Meg, 119

Saint-Exupéry, Antoine de, 81–82
same-sex marriage, 193
Sandra, 19–20, 184–85
saudade, 145
savoring, 148
Schultz, Connie, 157
scripts, 93–94
Second Lady, author as, 129–48
segregation, 33–34, 132
self, separation from, 31
self-acceptance, 197
self-actualization, 28–29
self-healing, 60
self-perception, 122
self-silencing, 8
self-worth, 100
sensitivity, high, 155, 164
separation from self, 31

sex trafficking, 90
sexual harassment, 44, 49
shame, 118, 120, 123
Shark Tank, 185
shipping containers, 102
SLOP, as nickname, 133
Smith, Jada Pinkett, 162, 164
soccer game, 191–92
social media, trolling and, 2–3
social norms, inverting, 165–68
social status
    caste system and, 55–56, 58
    shifts in, 34–35, 129–30
steel industry, 70, 72, 79, 88, 110
Stefanie, 178–79
Striking Gridiron (Nichols), 111
substance use
    addiction, 86, 137, 178–79
    alcohol dependency, 178
    increase in drug use, 137
    Narcan and, 104, 110, 137
    withdrawal in newborns, 67
sunflowers
    barricade for, 107–8
    planting of, 138
sweat equity, 67
swimming pools, 132–33
systemic inequities, 49–50

Telmo, Tio, 20, 139–40, 145, 147
Tippett, Krista, 147
tooth fairy, pandemic and, 139
toughness
    demand for, 31–32
    as perceived strength, 5–7
Trader Joe's, 105
traffic signs, mock, 100–101
traffic stop incident, 15
Traister, Rebecca, 159

trauma
children and, 199
description of, 59
effect of on behavior, 121
intergenerational, 35–36
personal, 59–60
trauma ghosting, 59
travel, during author's childhood, 21
trolling, 2–3
Trump, Donald, 141–42, 143
Twitter, Brazilian Carnival event
and, 134

Uncle Nick, 167
unconditional love, 124
unicorn, Build-a-Bear, 168
University of Pittsburgh Medical
Center, 97
unkindness, as response to pain,
37–38
urbanism, experimental, 70–71
U.S. House Judiciary Subcommittee
on Immigration and
Citizenship, 143

Vanderpump, Lisa, 171
Vanderpump Rules, 171
victim blaming, 32–33
Victim of the System (Fisher), 111
Vietnam War, 33
violence interruption work, 61–62

vulnerability
discomfort with, 33
as form of protection, 62
marginalization and, 205
public, 160–65
resistance to, 30–31

Walt, Mr., 172–73
Walter Reed Medical Center,
161, 162
welcomes, 18–19, 20
wellness checks, 101
Whatley, Demeatreas, 61
White House Correspondents'
Association Dinner, 171
Whitley, Drew, 111
Whole Foods, 105
Wilkerson, Isabel, 55–56, 58
Women in the Workplace
report, 50
Won't You Be My Neighbor? 35
workplace. *See* office environment
workplace/office environment, 48–49,
50–52
"worst wife" poll, 162, 164–65

yes, being first to, 183–89
yoga retreat, 70, 84
You Are Doing a Good Enough Job
(Lucido Johnson), 93
You've Got Mail, 119

Photograph of the author © Mara Rago

Gisele Barreto Fetterman is a Brazilian American activist, philanthropist, and nonprofit executive. She is the founder of the nonprofit Free Store 15104 and cofounder of the nonprofits For Good PGH and 412 Food Rescue. Her efforts have recovered millions of pounds of food and clothed several hundred thousand people. Fetterman was the first woman recipient of the Rodef Shalom Congregation's Pursuer of Peace Award. She currently resides in Braddock, Pennsylvania, with her husband, Senator John Fetterman, and their children.

CONNECT WITH GISELE BARRETO FETTERMAN ONLINE

X GiseleFetterman

⊙ GFett

ALWAYS FREE FROM MY LITTLE LIBRARY

LuvBooks

CHARTER # 180716